3.55

Paulji

A Memoir

By the same author
Hello Friend
A Journey in ECK

Paulji
A Memoir

Patti Simpson

ECKANKAR
Menlo Park, CA

Paulji
A Memoir
Copyright © 1985 Patti Simpson

The terms ECKANKAR, ECK, EK, SOUL TRAVEL, and VAIRAGI, among others, are trademarks of ECKANKAR, P.O. Box 3100, Menlo Park, CA 94026 U.S.A.

Printed in U.S.A.
ISBN: 0-88155-036-1
Library of Congress Catalog Card Number: 85-81716
Cover Design and Illustration by Stan Burgess

Second Printing 1986

For Gail and Helen, who were there then,
For David, who is here now,
and
For Paulji

Acknowledgements

I owe a special debt of gratitude to Rosalind Roberts Richards who transcribed over 150 hours of cassette tapes.

For assistance in areas so many they are uncountable, I also wish to thank Archie Hurst, Roger Dubin, and David Rivinus.

I would also like to thank others who, over the years, said yes quickly and always came through when asked for help. They are: Reggie, Ralph, Mike, and Michael from ECKANKAR's Audiovisual Department; Uli, Jim, and Steve for saintly patience in computer help; Sally McComb and Carol Morimitsu for photo research and endless encouragement; Joan Cross for archival and liaison assistance; Mark and Delene Harrison for organizing and simplifying boxes and drawers full of material; and last, but certainly not least, all the people who have shared so much with me over the years.

Preface

I t has been said that a history, to be properly written, should not be attempted until at least ten years have separated the writer from the event.

In the early 1970s I was not acquainted with that piece of wisdom, so I went about trying to write this story. I tried and tried and tried. It was like an amorphous article of clothing I couldn't figure out how to wear, despite trying it on every possible way — backwards, forwards, upside down, and inside out. It simply wouldn't work. What was solidly mine, however, was the knowledge that the story had to be written and that I was the one who had to do it.

Having exhausted all other possibilities, I decided to submerge the true story in a novel. It took three years to complete *The Moon Arrow*. The end result was a sharpening of the skills of my craft, meeting some interesting characters on

1

my pages, and having three years of peace feeling that I was finally fulfilling an obligation. I do not regret the three years spent on that first book. I learned much. But in the end, it was the wrong book and the wrong time, so I scrapped it.

For the student of the spiritual life, and for those with psychic abilities, timing can be a perplexity. "Who," "how," "why," and "where" can all be in place, but trying to understand "when" can drive one mad.

It has been fourteen years since Paul Twitchell, whom I call Paulji, died, or translated, from this plane of action. I do not know exactly why I couldn't write this story before, nor do I know why I am able to do it now, unless it is that old bugaboo, timing. One thing I do know: as it began to wend its way from my memory onto these pages, I could see the value of time's cushion. I saw something else too. While I am not always certain anymore of the exact sequence of some of my experiences with Paulji, the experiences themselves are crystal clear in every detail. No matter how many years have gone by, they still come out exactly the same. Often the phrases used are in the same wording I used fourteen years ago.

The novel I wrote was a fairly good one, but it didn't work because this is a true story. It is the story of a twentieth-century Adept and a normal, average housewife and mother who began to have mysterious and wonderful experiences; who, like Alice in Wonderland, began to grow too big for the room she was in.

Shortly before my adventures with Paulji began, I had discovered the author J.D. Salinger and had fallen in love with his writing. My favorite Salinger character was the poetic Seymour. In one book, Salinger had him commit suicide. I was furious with Salinger and wrote several letters to him in which I vented my anger and disappointment for such a travesty, but I never sent them. I remained disillusioned with Salinger until I began to grow too big for the room I was in. Then, suddenly, I understood. Outside of this human clay shell is so very much more to see. If I could just break out of this egg-like room I was squeezed into, I could *see more*. The day that understanding came — and I thought it in those exact words — I suddenly understood what Salinger had been trying to say and I forgave him.

As this story unfolds, it will become evident why I had such a close identification and interaction with that incident in Salinger's writing.

One

T he events described in this memoir began consciously for me in the summer of 1968. They revolve around the man known to the world as Paul Twitchell. Three years prior to that summer he had brought out the spiritual path, or teachings, that he called ECKANKAR, the Ancient Science of Soul Travel.

Today, millions of people around the world have heard or read something about ECKANKAR, and many thousands are enrolled in one or another of its study programs. But in the period I cover here, there were very few of us students, and fewer yet in that tiny cadre known as the Inner Circle.

I became one of the people in that circle, but to this day I cannot really understand why. I only know that for the first three decades of my life I was the most average, unremarkable person you could think of. I had a husband, four children, a few fears, an average education, and little ambition. I was relatively content with who I was, which was altogether conventional, right up to my politics and weekly attendance and involvement in my local Episcopal church.

Why me, of all people? I didn't know why then, and all these years later I still don't know the reason. The only thing I know for sure is that it did happen.

At a certain period in my life, I began to grow and have experiences in my inner consciousness that were, for me, unheard of. I began to find within myself a faculty I didn't know I had — inner guidance. At times this functioned like intuition, a feeling or a hunch that I would follow. At other times it bellowed at me or physically propelled me with unbelievable force, and I had no choice but to obey.

As I began to go along with this intuitive guidance, I discovered that there existed a whole body of experience and a cosmology that, over the centuries, many others had also found and written about. Perhaps of most importance to me is that I had these experiences first, then later found out what they were.

At times, I think that I was always going this way, slowly making my way to the point where I could find Paul Twitchell. At other times, I think that he found me. Whatever the truth is, I did meet, resist, accept, love, admire, and work for this remarkable being. In the physical world I also miss him. I sometimes feel that during the time he was in my life, I was a better person in some ways. I seemed to be smarter, stronger, faster, abler, and happier. Paulji illuminated all my good qualities and animated them. The fact that he was putting them all to work for his own purposes is beside the point. I wanted to help him. I wanted to experience the Patti he showed me I could be. Today I am not all that I was during that time, but I am far more than I was before we met, and that alone has made the journey worth my time.

To get an idea of how it all started, we need to go back to the summer of 1968.

* * *

The seashore where my family vacationed in June of that year was no more than thirty-five miles from our home, but it was like another world for me. As we drove away from the city and headed for the beach, I could feel all of my cares being left behind, as if I were shedding some dirty, tattered clothing. As the air became fresher and cleaner, so did my spirits. By the time we pulled our car into the driveway of our rented cottage, I was almost giddy with happiness. I supervised the unpacking and prepared a light supper; my husband, the children, and I then took a long stroll on the beach at sunset and retired early.

As I settled into my pillow that night, the elation I had felt earlier seemed to expand into a strange loosening or unwinding of tension. I had no idea what was happening or why, but it felt as if I had suddenly landed in ten feet of duck down and was sinking deeper and deeper into its enfolding softness. It seemed that no bed I had ever slept in had been exactly right until that moment. This bed knew me perfectly, and its sole purpose was to fit my body with such perfection that I could not tell where the bed stopped and I started.

What was happening was incredible! I usually rotate between three basic sleep positions and no others are comfortable. Now, to my delight, I found myself superbly comfortable in any position. I didn't have to shift but did, because no matter what position felt good, a new one felt even better. Every movement of my body filled me with pleasure. I realized that I had never felt so completely at one with my body. My body felt as if it were in perfect balance.

I seemed to be asleep as I languidly reflected on all this, and yet, I knew I was not really asleep because I was thinking about it in full awareness. My body was in a repose that resembled unconsciousness, yet I was fully aware of every one of its muscle fibers, of the bed, of the room, and of myself doing this strange thing and recording it.

When morning finally came I arose, to my knowledge never having lost consciousness the entire night. As the strange night had progressed, I recalled feeling concern about how this lack of sleep would affect me. However, once up and about, I was surprised to find that I felt more rested and refreshed than usual.

All day I wondered about the extraordinary night. How could I never have gone to sleep and yet feel so wonderfully refreshed? I was sure it must have been the new bed which was king-sized, because ours at home was a double. There must be a logical explanation.

The second night was an exact repeat of the first. I settled down and began to sink deeper and deeper into the glorious relaxation. Now two things were happening. I was aware of the delicious comfort and well-being of my physical body, and at the same time I was becoming aware of a sound, a seemingly disembodied voice, telling me things.

The "I" who was reveling in the pleasure of my body was also listening with rapt attention to the words being said. This "I" was thinking independently.

This information is marvelous. I must remember it.

When I awakened the next morning, however, what had been crystal clear and well understood was gone from my mind. I knew I'd heard wonderful things all night and remembered ordering myself to remember them, being certain I would, but I didn't. This was all the more puzzling because I was sure that, once again, I had not been asleep the entire night. Yet, surely, if I had been awake in the ordinary sense, I could never have forgotten the wondrous things I'd heard. Indeed, I had full memory of my body on the bed, of enjoying its relaxed positions, and of listening as the hours of the night passed.

Even though whatever it was that was going on

was inexplicable to me, it was not in the least disturbing. The deep relaxation of the body all night, in spite of no actual sleep, left me bubbling with life in the morning. The things I'd been told, but couldn't remember, left me with a sense of peace and happiness. Whatever was going on, I was definitely benefiting from it.

There was a similarity between these two nocturnal experiences and one I had had several years before. In the first one I had also seemed to be asleep, but awake in consciousness, and the words of a book had run through my head as if I were a tape recorder. It had been a most exciting and well-written mystery story, and as it unfolded, word by word, it left me fascinated. I didn't know where this mystery story was coming from; in a sense, it seemed to be from me. In the morning I couldn't remember a word of it, but I had a strange and profound understanding, a knowingness beyond a shadow of a doubt, that someday I would write a book.

This had been my first *Knowing,* and it was especially bizarre because I had never in my life thought about writing a book. I had been a mediocre writer in high school and college and had detested all the rules of grammar forced upon me.

The most interesting thing about a Knowing of this kind is that there is no doubt. It just is. I had never written anything—had never thought to. I didn't know how to write, nor had anything happened in my life to write about, but I knew I would someday write a book—also, that it would not be right away. There were some things to experience first, and it would be those things I would write about. I also knew something else. Never before, in my entire life, had I ever really known something. I had thought, wished, hoped, believed, trusted, and learned various things. But I hadn't known. Now, for the first time, I really knew one thing and knew it in spite of the lack of logic, reason, or any kind of authority.

One of the more remarkable aspects of all this was the patience with which I accepted the idea. I am usually very curious and excitable, and when presented with such an extraordinary idea, I should have been full of questions and testing. Ordinarily I would have wanted, above all, to be getting on with the writing immediately. But the Knowing inside of me said that some things would have to happen first, and I had utter and absolute confidence they would, although I had not even the tiniest hint as to their nature. That was part of it. Whatever I had to experience would happen. It could not be missed, for it was already mine. I had never been so sure, so totally secure, about anything in my life.

This Knowing was to drastically change the way I looked at a lot of things that I heretofore had regarded as facts. It first hit one Sunday morning in church as I was reciting the Apostles' Creed. Suddenly, I was mentally outside of myself and was listening very carefully to the things I was saying I believed. With chagrin I realized that of all those things I thought I believed—and my whole

11

spiritual viewpoint was based on them—I did not know that even one of them was true.

I don't *know* any of this stuff! I thought to myself.

Before it was over, my voice had left me; I just stood there wide-eyed, understanding more things than I could handle.

It was a revelation for me and also the beginning of the end. Before the year was out, I found more interesting things to do with my Sunday mornings than to go to church.

In both of these strange nocturnal instances— when I had heard the mystery story, and what was going on now—I was an alert observer or listener who was capable of independent thought. In both experiences I had charged myself to remember but couldn't, and in both, there was a complete absence of the symbols, pictures, and action that is the usual substance of dreams. There were also some dramatic differences between the two sets of nocturnal instances. The tremendous comfort of my body this time was new. The words of the book could have been from me, but this voice seemed "other" than me; and while the book had perhaps been an hour-long experience, the present one was continuing night after night.

After this nightly experience had been going on for well over two weeks, I had yet another sensation. I began to *feel* things about what was being told to me. Although I worked harder than ever at ordering myself to remember a certain piece of information, each morning it had slipped elusively from my grasp. Now I began to have a *sense* of what it was about.

I felt that I had been hearing the explanation of life, of existence. It was as if all life were some kind of giant clock, and that all of its functionings — the interrelating wheels, cycles, and gears — worked in harmony according to a master plan. It was, it seemed, truth. Truth was being told to me; truth more beautiful and wondrous than anything I could ever have conceived. The gears and wheels and their functions in this cosmic timepiece were being explained, and I could see that it worked perfectly.

While all of this was going on, I could think independently, but my thinking and reactions were always centered on telling myself to remember. My inner reaction to the information itself was total acceptance and neutrality; unlike my human self, I had no questions. There was no jumping ahead, no making of points, and no pondering. Whoever or whatever was the source of this information, it was impossible to question it, and there was absolutely no thought or desire to do so. There was nothing going on in me but my overwhelming sense of its rightness.

One thing that I often thought during the night and always remembered in the morning was this: If I can recall this when I awaken, I will never worry or feel anxiety or suffer again as long as I live. The damnable thing was, of course, I could never consciously remember any of it.

Although my nights were incredibly busy, and I hadn't slept in the ordinary sense for over two weeks, in my waking hours I had never looked or felt better. I seemed to possess the calm of a Buddha; a quality of inner peace and serenity pervaded my every thought and action. A friend who drove down from the city for a visit said, "There is something new about you, Patti. I don't know how to describe it, but the words 'poise' and 'grace' come to mind."

I smiled with appreciation. It was true, but I knew the source had to be kept to myself. There was not even the desire to discuss it, even with my husband; it was simply too unbelievable. So I hugged my secret to me and couldn't wait for night, when I could go to bed.

On two occasions I had daytime visions that seemed to be connected with the night's instructions. One morning I awoke and experienced the visual image of Saul of Tarsus—St. Paul. On the road to Damascus, he was knocked to the ground and struck blind by a flash of light. I knew, though not how I knew, exactly what had happened there—how and why it had come about. The fact that I couldn't explain it with words didn't seem to matter. It was simply an encapsulated moment in history that had a very logical, reasonable explanation along the lines of those teachings which lay within me, just beyond the reach of the mind and tools of language. In view of what happened later, I would say, with

14

hindsight, that the phenomenon known as "divine intervention" is a genuine, physical-world experience.

The second vision came in the form of a river. I have told about this in my earlier book, *Hello Friend,* but will repeat it here. In this vision I saw that all life, consciousness, and experience is like a river that flows inexorably to its destination— the sea. What the sea was, I was not sure, but I had a hunch that if any of us seek a goal or a desti-nation, it is to be found at this sea. For me, the goal was largely undefined, but it had to do with all the teachings of the world's great spiritual leaders.

Since I was most familiar with the Christian religion, I superimposed the teachings of Christ over the vision of the river. I knew he understood the river, that he was trying to show his followers how to navigate it and make their way to the sea. I also saw a misunderstanding or mistake about those teachings because, in Christianity, there is the element of failure: the warning that if one makes certain mistakes, he does not get to the sea. I saw that this is not at all how it is. One is in the river and goes where the river goes; it is that sim-ple. Of course, one may, as a leaf or a twig, become caught in eddies and sidepools, but these are mere diversions. Eventually, the current picks one up again and the journey to the sea continues.

At this juncture I had yet another revelation. I realized that though one can swim against the current, or sideways to it, and even though tremendous energy and effort may be expended, the force and pull of the current will inevitably bring one to the goal. If one understands there is a destination and comprehends the nature of the river, then it is not necessary to strain and try so hard, to flail about and worry. It was so clear, I was stunned. One just relaxes and floats effortlessly to the sea.

Running parallel to this vision of the river was a giant question in my mind: What of death?

As I posed this question to my vision, I was shown where it fit; it was in tune with the river. I saw that, in reality, destruction is a meaningless concept. Forms are born, live, and die, then are reborn into new forms. The basic plot of existence is death and rebirth, the phoenix rising from the ashes. Things are torn down, but other things take their places. If one's philosophy is that good dies out and is replaced by evil, then one need only await the inevitable: Evil will in turn die out and again be replaced by good.

Yet I saw that this concept didn't fit the vision. In the river the terms good and evil were not real. The only reality was the flow of the current to the great sea. I saw that the birth and death of forms did not hold the essence of construction and destruction so much as their *rearrangement*. The vision stopped my worry about death, although I would not have a Knowing about reincarnation until another year had passed.

The dream teachings, as I came to call them, went on for twenty-one unbelievable nights, leaving me enchanted. Vast realizations were coming to me about the nature of things, and at the same time I wondered, what is this voice that is filling my nights with all this wonderful information? The voice had no character; it seemed to be a very impersonal reciting of information, almost like a machine. There was never the slightest amount of interplay between it and me; it spoke, I listened.

On the twenty-first day, I arose with the definite idea that there was a book I needed to find. I had no idea *what* book or even of the subject. It was simply the inner knowingness that I must go out and find a book today.

I drove to a small corner market about half a mile from the beach and walked in. Locating the paperback rack, I spun the carousel and browsed.

Studying the titles, I awaited the impulse that would connect me with something I saw, but nothing happened. I went over every title but nothing moved inside me. My intuition told me I was in the right place; the book was here. Yet, my usually effective, intuitive selection process seemed to have deserted me. Unwilling to leave without the book, I shifted into my mental gear and studied the titles again. I would just have to pick the one that seemed most interesting. This was a more difficult method of selection for me, and when I finally decided upon one, I wasn't at all sure it was the right one.

I turned to take the book to the checkstand, feeling sure it was not right. I had only taken two steps when, out of the corner of my eye, I caught a glimpse of another book carousel hidden in a corner of the market. I moved quickly to the second rack and began to spin it. Suddenly, my hand shot out and grabbed a book. It was *In My Soul I Am Free* by Brad Steiger. The cover said it was "the biography of the amazing Paul Twitchell." Paul Twitchell, I said to myself laughing, what a funny name. Nevertheless, I bought the book.

That night the dream teachings stopped.

The book about Paul Twitchell lay, unread, on the coffee table for a week. Strangely uneasy about it, I would walk by and look at it lying there; rather than read it, I would read anything else I could find. The book disturbed me. It was almost as if there might be something in it that could upset me. Each night I approached sleep with the hopeful thought that the wonderful dream teachings would return, but in vain. Each day, I walked past the book which, though unread, had the odd power to annoy me. Finally, telling myself how silly all this was, I picked it up. I looked at the smiling picture of Paul Twitchell on the cover and thought, What could this pleasant-looking man possibly have to say that could upset my life in any way? I read the book.

As I read along, it seemed I was involved in a very odd coincidence. What the book was saying appeared to be closely connected with some of the things I had retained from the many nights of dream teaching. A month ago I would have found

18

much of what was being said to be incomprehensible and totally foreign. However, because I had had those realizations, a lot of what this man, Paul Twitchell, said, made sense. On the last page was an address where people could write to him for more information on his philosophy. Part of me wanted to find out more; another part was wary. Still another part was just plain terrified. This last part ruled, and I decided not to write to him. My conviction wavered, however, as the days passed and the dream teachings still didn't return. Finally, I had to face facts. It was more than mere coincidence that the dream teachings stopped the very day I had bought the book. This must have been a signal or an omen. Perhaps if I contacted the man, the dream teachings would return.

I sat down and carefully composed a letter to Paul Twitchell. If he were, indeed, responsible for my wonderful nocturnal happenings, he would know from what I wrote, who I was and what had gone on. Then, having composed my very best effort, I sent it off and sat back to see what he would do with my great secret. Two weeks later a letter came from his office. With a slight tremble that betrayed my anxiousness, I tore it open. It was a form letter.

I found this disgusting. Once again I vowed to have nothing to do with him, but I did keep the order form. Even though I worked diligently at ignoring it, it was a losing game, because the dream teachings never returned.

Finally, I gave up and decided to write a letter signing on for a year of his discourses. On the one hand I gave in, but on the other, I wanted to be very firm with him about the fact that I had just awakened from a lifetime of believing things that I didn't *know,* and even if he might have some things of interest to teach me, I was not about to get into some weird philosophy. I wanted to hear more but would not believe blindly in anything ever again. I would read what he had to say, but before believing any of it, he'd first have to prove it to me. I would have to *know* it. Little did I realize that this was precisely the kind of contract he liked best.

It took exactly a year for him to prove what he promised: that "after a year of study, the chela will look around and scarcely recognize his life."

During that year we had made a completely unscheduled move thirty-five miles from the smoggy Los Angeles suburb we lived in, down to the beach where we usually vacationed. Everything in this physical environment was completely new, different, and perfect for me. And yet, during that year I had been a defiant Doubting Thomas. I did not give Paul Twitchell even one little break.

About midway through my first year of study, a notice came that Paulji was to be in Los Angeles for one evening at the Biltmore Hotel, and he was holding a meeting for chelas (students) only. I decided to go, just to see what he looked like.

That evening I was in high gear to rip him to

20

shreds. My critical eye was sharpened to a stiletto point. When he walked into the room, I noticed that he was short, perhaps five foot five or six inches. He was dressed all in blue and his clothes were a bit rumpled. His hair was rather long for a gentleman of his years, which I judged to be about fifty-five or sixty. The nicest thing about him was his aquiline nose and very firm, square jaw. He had a habit, as he talked, of fiddling with his wristwatch. Often he'd remove it completely, then put it back on, only to remove it once more.

The real problem though was when he spoke; he seemed to have no regard for the English language. His accent was Southern with a British twist, a dialect I later learned occurs in parts of Kentucky which is where he was originally from.

Although I did manage to find fault with him—enough to allow me to remain feeling free of his influence—I did get pinned to my seat once by a particularly powerful look he shot into the audience. He had been discussing the fact that we, as seekers, had a lot of excess baggage to throw overboard, mainly in the areas of our opinions and mindsets. Since that was where I was operating from, he nailed me well. I was therefore fairly uncomfortable at the intense look he had sent in my direction.

The only really compelling part of the whole evening was when he walked off the dais and into a circle of people who were obviously his chelas. I saw something that is difficult to describe: an aura or circle of love so strong it appeared to be lighter than the rest of the room, an almost solid thing to the naked eye. For a moment I was captured by something I didn't understand, something beautiful, something I was not a part of. For that moment, for that one instant, I felt a strange longing but quickly passed it off and hurried from the place, still hanging onto the mindset: I want no part of this.

As is often the case with me at big moments in my life, I am given a dream that moves me deeply. This also happened shortly before my first year of study was up.

I seemed to be in a beauty spa or some kind of a resort and was in a line with a lot of other women. We were walking to a pool which apparently was part of the self-improvement regimen. One by one those ahead of me marched into the pool, which was not much of a pool; it was shallow and had a mud bottom. Once in, the women reached down and grabbed up handfuls of mud and smeared it all over their naked bodies.

I was watching this as my turn approached and realized that although we'd been told that this would make us beautiful, it was a lie, some kind of a trick, a desecration. I knew that when my turn came, I would be expected to go through the same stupid ritual the others were. However, I — the dreamer — turned out to be a far stronger individual than the waking, everyday Patti, and I said to myself, Oh no, there is no way I am going to follow this mindless herd of sheep. With great

22

independence and a panache that Patti, the dreamer, found utterly delightful, I made a high, arching, graceful dive into the water, skimming into it so lightly that I avoided the mud.

Immediately following my rebellion in the pool, I found myself under a hair dryer. A butler-type man handed me the bill for my treatment at the beauty spa. I don't recall the figure, but I gasped. What a scam! Once again the fierce independence came over me. I indignantly said to the man, "I will not pay this price. It is not worth it. I will pay you exactly what it's all worth!" With that I hastily scratched out a check for a meager $15.00. He didn't argue. Instead, he led me to a secret door that opened into another part of the place.

This was amazing. The people who were trying to get beautiful with the mud were completely unaware of this door, and of the very different world beyond it. This new place was nothing like the circus I'd just left. It was quiet and peaceful here, and the beauty was real, not the artificially-induced glamour of the spa.

I was wrapped in a huge, soft, white towel. Though still not completely dry from my swim over the top of the mudbath, I was very clean. I walked into a light, airy room filled with fragrant tropical plants. Toward the back, in another room, was a group of people, also freshly bathed and wrapped in the fluffy towels. They were sitting in a semicircle on the floor. Seated in a chair, facing them, was a very old man, dressed in a long white robe. He was a teacher or a guru and he was talking about the place.

"Very few of those who visit out there find the door to this place. They waste all their time and money on foolishness which they think will bring them beauty. They are so busy with outer appearances that they never find this sanctuary, which is where true beauty is born — the beauty of the inner spirit."

I was also sitting at the old man's feet, having joined the others to listen to his wisdom. Suddenly, I was overcome with love for this great Soul, whoever he was, because I knew he spoke Truth.

When I awakened from that dream, I had a feeling it had been a recap of my whole life on earth. I thought about the secret room and the great Soul teaching in it, about the joyous independence I had exhibited — marveling that I had a self in me like that. I had never met that Patti before, I liked her. I also realized that I was growing into her because of one thing: Paul Twitchell and his teachings.

So, in one year, one short year, I had looked inside myself and found a free spirit. Outside myself was a new home, a beautiful place by the sea. In that moment, I was sure that I owed all of that to Paulji. I then remembered what an awful student I had been — so doubtful, so critical, such a terrible brat — and burst into tears of shame. I felt that all this time he had been working, working, working at the inner core of my life, just as he had said he would, and I had given him nothing but a hard time. How could I ever make it up to him? Would he ever forgive me?

At that moment of surrender, I experienced what is called the Presence of the Master. I was suddenly surrounded by unconditional love. It was a palpable, fluid substance that encompassed me — warming, holding, and assuring me beyond all measure of doubt that I had no need for remorse or shame. It didn't matter. Nothing in the past mattered. All Paulji cared about was what I knew right now. From that day on, I called him my spiritual Master; and myself, "chela."

Two

_____

I t was early morning. First light was just
beginning to creep through the curtains
in my bedroom, and I was basking in the twilight
zone between sleep and waking. Suddenly, I heard
a voice—loud, deep, and masculine. It jolted me.
I thought it came from somewhere in the room, but
just before opening my eyes, I realized that it was
in my head.

"You are to purchase ten canvases," it said.

"You mean the kind you paint on?" I asked, stirring with great excitement. In an instant, I
realized that I must be having my first communication with a spiritual traveler, one of those great
beings who assist spiritual seekers on the inner
planes.

"Exactly. You are to purchase ten blank canvases."

At last. At last. I had been hoping for such a
long time to make the acquaintance of one of these

fellows. This one was definitely not Paulji, because the voice didn't have a Southern accent, but it didn't matter. We could still talk over my deep questions in a nice inner dialogue.

"Okay, I'll do it. After I get them, then what will I do with them?"

"That will be revealed to you at the proper time."

"Well, what is the purpose for this?" I wanted to get this out of the way so we could get on to one of the deep dialogues.

Silence.

"Hello? Are you still there?"

Silence.

He was gone. Not very nice of him, I thought. The least he could do after asking me to carry out something so outrageous was to sit around and chat for awhile about the universes or something. By now I was wide awake and thinking about ten canvases.

I do not paint. I had no idea why the inner guide would make such a crazy request. Is it a test to see if I will trust the inner experience, I pondered, to surrender to it even when it seems frivolous or outrageous? No problem. It's bizarre, but I shall trust it.

The next week I spent running my car about town, exhausting the meager supplies of stretched canvases available. Some were quite large, but when I found one, I bought it, regardless, until I had ten. Then I sat back, awaiting a further visit from the stranger who had given these directions. Nothing. Days went by, then weeks. Day after day

I looked at the empty canvases, which were stacked all over the house, and waited. Finally, I decided the fellow was not going to return, and I had better go to work on them myself. I took my question into contemplation. What in the world am I going to do with ten canvases? I didn't get a proper answer. All I got was a subtle impression: "Express what is going on in your inner worlds in any way you want." Lacking any other inspiration, this is what I did.

Most often, I started out with a black canvas. To one I added a tiny white figure looking up at a vast starry universe. Then I did collages with glue and tissue. On another one I rolled white paint around in a glob on a stark black canvas — a bird. They were, basically, pretty awful, but eventually I filled up ten. Then they sat there, huge paintings propped up all over the house. The family was beginning to complain. But I didn't know what came next, so I waited. Then one day a letter arrived from the ECKANKAR office that said the Third World Wide Seminar of ECKANKAR would be in Los Angeles in October. For the first time there would be a chela art exhibition. The only stipulation was that the art be spiritual in nature. The letter was signed by a lady named Helen Baird.

I sat thinking about this for a long time. Could it possibly be that this art show was what all those paintings were about? I seemed to qualify in that I was a chela and had chosen spiritual experiences to paint.

I will share my whole experience with Helen, I thought, and maybe she'll tell me if this art exhibit is what it was all about. I sat down and wrote a letter to her.

Before long Helen wrote back, saying that my letter had moved her deeply, and yes, please, by all means, bring the art to the World Wide.

Then, as if I had satisfactorily completed that cycle, a new one presented itself. In my now regular contemplation I heard Paulji say very clearly to me, "I want to see you at the seminar; I have something to give you."

Oh dear, it was getting tougher by the moment. I thought about it. The only thing that came to mind was the *Mystic World* notice that Paulji would give consultations at the seminar to those who wrote and requested them.

Well, I thought, I should write and request one. And so I did. Soon a card came back from the ECKANKAR office saying that I should see the appointment secretary when I arrived at the seminar.

I was terribly excited in the days before my first seminar. I would be getting rid of all these canvases cluttering up the house and also hear Paulji talk for the first time, with the conscious awareness of who he was to me. In addition, I was going to meet my new friend Helen Baird, with whom I was now exchanging enthusiastic letters several times a week, and would probably meet Paulji in person, in a consultation.

This last possibility had me very jumpy as I understood that, in a consultation, one brought one's problems to the Master. My only problem was that I had no problem to tell him, and so the last days were spent in searching for one, for some excuse to relate to him when we met. I feared I would have to make something up and must have run through at least two hundred scenarios. One that never occurred to me was to tell him the truth, that he came to me on the inner and said he wanted to see me, that he had something for me.

The big day came. I loaded up a station wagon with my ten framed canvases and arrived at the International Hotel near the Los Angeles airport. I found Helen, and she helped unload them. It was pretty funny, actually. Helen had been exposed to somebody's wonderful inner experience — a chela being instructed by one of *them*, a great ECK Master, to do ten canvases. Surely, these canvases were going to be earth- and heaven-shattering. When she looked at them, her disappointment was written all over her face. It was comical, watching her trying to recover and be gracious with me. Her comment was something like, "Oh, uh, they're very primitive, aren't they?" Sometimes the gap between the inner ideal and the outer manifestation can be embarrassing, but I was trusting it all and thus remained unruffled.

So many things happened at that seminar that, in retrospect, I feel it must have been several seminars at once. All of it couldn't possibly have happened in the space of that one short weekend.

One thing that most frightened me was when Helen told me of a poetry competition. Since I had sent several poems to the office in the past, I was entered, and was expected to read one of them in the program. I flatly refused.

I had a terror about speaking in front of audiences. Several years ago, before I left the Episcopal church, our local parish had given a going-away party for our priest, a man who had been a special friend to me and of whom I was very fond. One of the organizers asked me to say a few words, and although I truly loved this priest and had grown tremendously during his stay with our congregation, I could not overcome my fear and do what was requested. Finally they gave me the chore of going to the microphone and giving the attendees some simple instructions as to how they would proceed in the food lines. I practiced it for days.

When the big moment came for me to deliver my two lines, my stomach knotted with fear, the palms of my hands were wringing wet, and my lips were quivering so violently that I could barely stammer out the words. Even so, I got mixed up and didn't say it right.

Read a poem? To an audience of strangers? To anyone? It was unthinkable. Helen pulled out her big gun.

"Paul has requested that the chelas whose poems are in the competition read them. Period." This was my first experience with the impact of a request from Paulji.

One of the most puzzling things about the seminar was when I contacted the appointment secretary for the consultation. He shook his head and said that it was impossible, that Paulji had been booked solid for six months. I showed him the postcard I was sent. He laughed and shook his head again.

"I have no idea why you were sent this. It's impossible."

I was somewhat relieved as I still had not found a satisfactory problem to present to Paulji, but I was also confused about the cancelled consultation. I had never had that strong, inner voice be wrong. It always turned out right, no matter what, if I would just trust it. Oh well. I was truly disappointed that I would not meet Paulji in person. But I swallowed it and concentrated on the panic of having to read a poem to the seminar audience.

Saturday morning I was sitting in the auditorium listening to an interesting talk. Suddenly, yet another strange feeling swept over me.

I cannot sit in this room another minute, I thought. I have to get out of here.

The feeling had been unbelievably strong. I got up quickly, and quietly eased out the door and into the hallway. I stood there, utterly confused.

Well, I said inwardly to whomever or whatever had propelled me out of there, you got me out, now what?

No answer. I was really getting annoyed with this inner stuff. It seemed to give you just enough to get you started, then left you in a puddle of confusion. Nothing came from my intuition, so I switched into mental gear.

I didn't have time for breakfast earlier, I thought, so I guess I'll go down to the coffee shop and get something to eat. I was annoyed because I had been very interested in the talk in the auditorium, but I left anyway because of the inner prompting.

I walked into the coffee shop and took a seat. The waitress brought a menu, which I studied for a few minutes, and then she took my order. It was only then that I looked up, straight into the face of the appointment secretary, who was sitting two tables away. He was intensely involved in a conversation with a man whose back was to me, but who was dressed all in blue, was a bit in need of a haircut, and whom I recognized immediately. Boy, oh boy, oh boy! My knees went weak and my heart began to beat like a drum. There he sits—Paulji—so close I could simply walk over there and . . . Well, that would be impolite. I thought, gee, if only the appointment secretary would look over here and see me, perhaps he would recall my problem, call me over, and I could at least say hello.

With this in mind, I began frantically trying to catch the eye of the secretary. I waved, grinned, winked. He didn't see me. I became more assertive. Telepathically, I sent him the message: Hey, look here, over here. Remember me? Call me over. Hey, look over here.

But he wouldn't. And I was so naive! Here I was sending this highly charged message right over the head of probably the most psychically sensitive man I was ever to meet. It's a wonder he could carry on a conversation with all the noise passing through his head.

Obviously, sending telepathic messages wasn't going to work. I sank back into my seat in despair and gave up bombarding the man. Then it came again, the inner voice which was steadily getting me into more and more trouble.

"Nobody's going to do this for you, Patti. This is something you have to do for yourself."

Oh dear. I knew I had to stand up and go over to him. I tried, but there were no bones in my legs. I was a blob, stuck to the chair. Then I looked up and saw several women walk by, stop at the table to greet Paulji, and chat awhile before walking on. Soon two more came in and did the same, and he invited them to sit in the empty seats beside him and the secretary.

Look at that! I said to myself. It's okay, others do it, Patti. All you have to do is get up and do it.

I made three attempts to stand. My palms were soaking wet. My knees would raise me two or three inches from the seat, then collapse. Time was running out, I realized, and I was not going to get it done. I was . . . a coward. I was angry with myself but was already making really good rationalizations, when, to my utter astonishment, something seemed to literally kick me in the seat, into a standing position. I was halfway to Paulji's

35

table before my mind registered what was happening, and then it was too late. I was there.

Immediately he stood up, took my outstretched hand in both of his, and I was looking into the most intense, electric blue eyes I have ever seen in my life.

"Hello, Paulji," I stammered, "I just wanted to introduce myself. I'm Patti Simpson, one of your chelas."

"How do you do, Patti; I'm very glad to meet you."

His face was incredibly kind. He squeezed my hand in both of his, but then he seemed to wander in his attention. He looked puzzled for a moment, and he stopped looking into my eyes. Instead, he began to search a spot right above my head, as if he were reading the air there. I was suddenly overwhelmed with the feeling that I was standing in a brilliant spotlight, stark naked. I felt completely vulnerable. There was not one piece of information about myself that I could hide from this individual. He knew everything about me, including things I didn't even know myself. It was very unpleasant.

A frown of puzzlement crossed his face. "Did you try to see me?" he asked. "Did you want . . . a consultation?"

"Yes," I said, amazed. "I tried to get an appointment, but you didn't have any more time open."

"Yes, I know I'm all booked up, but maybe I can . . ."

Perhaps it was the discomfort of that search-light, or maybe it was Soul talking, but suddenly I said, "No, no, that's all right, I really don't need an appointment. I think I understand now," which, of course, I didn't.

"You're sure?" he asked kindly.

"I'm quite sure," I said, without the slightest inkling of what I was talking about. And with that, I thanked him and left. I spun out of the room in a daze, never giving a thought to the breakfast I had ordered. Something inside me was giving way, and it was difficult to hang onto my composure. I was walking away from there so fast, I was almost running. Making a right turn, I was at the door of the art exhibit room.

There stood Pat Henderson, a lady I had met earlier and had instantly liked. I blurted out, "I just met Paulji," and then, inexplicably, I burst into tears. Pat put her arms around me and hugged me and laughed. I was convulsed with huge, wet sobs.

"I can't understand why I'm crying," I told her in between sobs, "I'm not unhappy."

Pat seemed to laugh all the harder. She patted me. "What's happened is that you've experienced the *darshan*," she laughed.

"What's that?"

"The Meeting with the Master. The reason you're crying is because you've probably been working for it for thousands of lifetimes."

The tears I shed were not tears of joy or pain. They felt like relief. Although I felt silly, I also felt very much like a child who had been lost in the forest but had finally been found. Pat's comment made sense. I felt that I would never forget the intensity and the detail of meeting the Master as long as I lived.

It was only after Pat had explained what had taken place that I understood what Paulji had meant when he had told me on the inner to see him, that he had something for me. And I understood why I had inexplicably turned him down and refused to allow him to make an adjustment in his schedule so that I could have a consultation. Without mentally knowing it I, Soul, understood that the gift had been given, although I, the human, hadn't the faintest idea what was going on.

After that, things really began to heat up. Helen, all out of breath, came running up to me.

"I've been looking everywhere for you. Do you know that collage-painting of yours that shows the Master and chela walking through a dark forest?"

"Yes?"

"Well, Brad Steiger was in the artroom a little while ago and fell in love with it; he wants to buy it. But I didn't know if you wanted to sell it, or if so, how much you wanted for it."

I was stunned. Brad Steiger. The man who wrote *In My Soul I Am Free,* the book that changed my life, wanted to buy one of *my* paintings? It was obvious that Helen was as stunned as I was — or more. Especially since there were many really excellent paintings in the artroom.

Helen said that Brad had gone to get his wife. I reached into the ethers and pulled out a price tag of $35. Unbelievable. I had met Paulji, and now Brad Steiger was going to buy one of my crazy pictures.

I managed to get through the rest of the seminar, though in a daze, and even through the poetry reading. At the rehearsal I was so terrible that the folks felt pity for me. My largest problem was that I raced through the poem like a radio announcer who has to squeeze too much copy into a thirty-second spot. They had me do it two or three times, but it didn't get better. One man, Stan, a tall, kind gentleman, who later became a dear friend, was playing his recorder in the program. I finally asked him if he would mind playing very slowly behind me, and perhaps this would aid me in pacing myself. He agreed.

Nevertheless, as my moment approached, I was terrified. I sat there, trying to hold off the passing minutes, braced in a defensive skid against time. I trembled visibly. When my turn came, I simply could not, of myself, do it, and I knew it. So I did the only thing I could. I went inside myself to find the inner Paulji, and said, Look, I can't do this, so, since you seem to want it, you do it for me.

I was doing the thing we call "turning it over to Spirit, or to the ECK." To my delight the poetry reading went okay. Those readers who have recently seen me talk to audiences in huge convention centers around the world may be surprised to

39

discover how much shyness Paulji helped me to overcome.

I ran into Paulji twice more in the hallways. He always said, "Hello, Patti." What an amazing memory, I thought.

Brad Steiger never did come back for the painting, but it didn't matter. He had liked it. Apparently, his wife had not. I donated my ten masterpieces to ECKANKAR to sell, if they could, and said they could keep any of the proceeds. One thing I was not interested in was hauling them all back home.

A week or so after the seminar I received a letter from Helen. Once again she was in a state of excitement.

"It seems," she wrote, "that your little painting of the Master and the chela was Gail Twitchell's favorite of all the hundreds she saw, and she asked Paul if she could have it. I told him I thought you would be delighted to give it to Gail, but he insists on paying you for it."

I could scarcely believe my eyes.

I wrote back to her immediately. "Helen, I will not hear of Paulji paying me for that painting. It is my gift to Gail. Please tell him that, and as far as I'm concerned, he can have my paints, my brushes, my easel, and the ground it stands on. I owe him everything. It's too small a gift."

I went around grinning and shaking my head for days. All these things had happened to me — all these wonderful things — because I had trusted that crazy voice that told me to get ten canvases. It was a lesson to last me a lifetime: seeing what

40

could happen if one trusted the inner voice, no matter how silly it seemed at the time.

Three

I hurried through a light rain to pick up the day's mail. Among the letters was a blue envelope from the ECKANKAR office in Las Vegas, my name typed neatly on the front. I assumed it was an announcement or brochure and opened the other mail first. Then I opened the blue one. It was a letter which began, "Dear Patti:" The next line caused a jolt of energy to shoot through me: "I would very much like to thank you for the gift of the painting to Gail and myself."

I was holding a letter from Paulji, himself! There was so much energy and magic surrounding anything to do with this man. Everything concerning him seemed supercharged and electrifying. In the months and years to come, I would be receiving hundreds of these blue letters from him, but the energy they contained and evoked in me never diminished.

When I recovered, I read on: "Perhaps at some

time in the future, I shall be able to repay you with some spiritual favor. Yours truly, Paul Twitchell."

Repay me? I was incredulous. Why would he want to repay me, when it was I who was eternally in his debt for all he was giving me, in both my outer and inner life? This vexing situation is one I have never solved to this day, and I am often confronted with it. Sometimes, when a reader has been especially moved or touched by something in *Hello Friend,* he or she will write to me expressing gratitude. I always want to say, "Oh, but it is *I* who am grateful — that I found ECKANKAR, that I was able to write the book, and that I receive such beautiful letters from wonderful people all over the world." I feel I can never adequately express my thanks for all of this — and yet, people are thanking me.

I still have not put it all together, how that works, but I first saw it working in something else that happened to me at that eventful Third World Wide Seminar.

While walking down a hallway carrying a copy of Paulji's newest book, I began to get one of those strange feelings that something big and important was about to happen. Suddenly, I felt very warm, very tense, and very alert. The trusty inner voice said, "Turn around, turn around and look behind you." I turned. There, walking all alone, jaunty and smiling, was Paulji. Gracious, my cup was certainly running over. I stopped, waited for him to catch up, and smiled a shy hello.

"Are you enjoying the seminar, Patti?" he asked.

I was so happy that he remembered my name that I found it difficult to answer him. Finally, I murmured, "Oh yes, I'm having a great time, thank you."

"Good," he said.

We were each about to move on when I had an idea.

"Paulji, would you mind autographing your new book for me?"

He smiled, took the book from me, removed a black, felt-tipped pen from his coat pocket and wrote something in it. Then he handed the book back to me and said, "Thank you, Patti." I started to laugh, and for the first but not the last time I corrected him: "Oh no, Paulji, it is *I* who thank *you*." He raised an eyebrow and looked at me with mild amusement, much as one might regard an exuberant puppy.

I walked away, lost in thought. How really odd, he does me a favor, then thanks me. I could only assume it meant he was thanking me for the opportunity to do a favor. It was mind-boggling. I had difficulty comprehending this degree of humility.

The phenomenon of the strange sensation that always encompassed me whenever Paulji was in my physical vicinity is another matter that was to be unique in my experiences with him. Whenever he entered a seminar room, or even when he was walking down the hall toward it, I had the same feeling I described before. I did not have to turn around in my seat and look to know he was there. Soul knew. Soul always knew when he was near, except, I assume, when he didn't want to be seen.

I recall one morning at a later seminar, Helen and I were seated in a coffee shop having breakfast. We had been sitting there eating and jabbering for the better part of an hour when, suddenly, we saw Paulji get up from the counter across from us and approach our table. He smiled and said, "Good morning, ladies. How are you this morning?" Both of us were dumbfounded that we hadn't seen him sitting there. I was particularly so, because usually my sensory perception clanged bells and flashed lights whenever he was within half a block. Later I was to learn that if he didn't want to be bothered, he would simply mockup that he was invisible, and there was absolutely no way you would notice him; since it was his desire for privacy, my Soul self, who could easily find him, left him alone and sent my human mechanism no messages.

A few months after Paulji wrote the thank-you letter, I received a letter from Helen stating that he would be in the Los Angeles area in January, and that he would like to give me the Second Initiation at that time. I was thrilled and knew that this must be the spiritual favor he had spoken of, as I was still some months away from completing two years of study.

The night before the initiation I had a strange dream. I was sitting at an outdoor cafe, perhaps in Paris. There were many people about. Suddenly I heard someone shout. I looked around. The people were shouting and pointing. I looked too, and there, high on a rooftop, stood a woman. It was obvious she was about to jump. And in a few moments she did, plummeting eerily to her death in the street below. The crowd screamed in horror and anguish.

I, myself, watched in curious detachment, not at all horrified. But I told myself, as I watched the grim tableau, I know exactly how that feels. I, the dreamer, was puzzled at my total lack of emotion about the whole matter and also puzzled at the texture of this dream—because I was both the dreamer and also the totally conscious entity, Patti. It was indeed a very strange dream.

The next day I left my home at the beach hours before the appointment with Paulji. I wanted to be sure I didn't get hung up in traffic. It had rained much of the night, and now the sky was filled with huge, billowy cumulus clouds. The sun played peekaboo with the clouds and often sent shafts of light piercing down through them in a Cecil B. DeMille celestial extravaganza that today seems to me may have been a bit overdone, but it was most appropriate to the me I was then, and for the day it happened to be, and my mission. It made the drive go by quickly and filled me with enchantment.

I arrived in the lobby of the hotel an hour and a half before I was due to see Paulji. So I sat and looked out the window at the lovely gardens and enjoyed being in the same building he was in. It was funny though, I didn't feel the same sensation that had come over me at the seminar in October.

The hour and a half seemed like five, and I was a little sorry I had been so anxious to be early because I was very bored. I began hoping that perhaps in his omniscience, Paulji would realize I was already there and maybe he would come down looking for me sooner than the appointed time. He didn't, though, and so I people-watched and enjoyed the garden. All of a sudden the familiar feeling came over me: he's here, he's here. I turned and looked around the lobby but didn't see him. Then something caught my attention at the lobby entrance. The doors were glass and through them I saw the doorman opening the door of a car. Out stepped Paulji, big as life. I had to laugh. No wonder I hadn't felt anything special; he wasn't even here.

I hurried over and greeted him with a big, exuberant hug. He excused himself for a moment and went over to the reception desk to get his room key and messages. Then together we entered the elevator and went up the seventeen floors to his rooms. An experience occurred in the elevator that was, in some ways, to affect a certain area of our dealings with each other ever after.

As the elevator began its ascent, Paulji seemed to drift away in his thoughts, as if reminiscing or being far, far away. Very quietly, not even looking at me, but at this far-off vision, he said, "It's been a long, long time, Patti . . . a long time . . . " I, thinking he was referring to when last we met, which was October, corrected him for the second time in our brief acquaintance. Laughing, I said, "Well, Paulji, it's only been three months." When I said this, it seemed to jar him out of his reverie. He shook his head as if to recover himself into present time.

"Oh," he said with kindness, "was I mumbling absentmindedly?"

I didn't know what to say, so I laughed and told him what he had just said, my inference being, of course, that he had made a rather humorous mistake. He regarded me with a look I simply cannot describe.

"Please forgive me," he said, "I do that sometimes."

By now some vague awareness was beginning to creep over me that he had been referring to something else, and that it was I who had misunderstood his meaning and had made a big mistake. The extent of the mistake would come home to me again and again, whenever I tried to uncover more of the memory beyond this time to find the roots of this old and beautiful bond between us. Many times I, alone, or in conversations with him, would be right at the edge of knowing; it was so close I could feel it there, but I was never allowed to have it. The knowledge of any past associations between us was closed to me for this lifetime, and there is absolutely no doubt in my mind that it is because when this fragile reality began to issue forth from him, when he began to touch upon it, I was insensitive to it. It was the first in a series of lessons I would learn about keeping myself detached, watchful, and low-key around him. I do not remember one of these lessons to be without pain or, often, acute embarrassment.

We entered the sitting room of his suite. There were large picture windows running across the opposite wall, and due to last night's rains, also an unusually breathtaking view of the San Bernardino Mountains. They were beautiful and seemed close enough to touch. I ran to the window to look at them, then automatically looked down to the sidewalk, seventeen stories below. Quickly I sucked in my breath and jumped back. I had been cursed all my life with a fear of heights. Looking down like that always made me nauseous.

"Is something wrong?" Paulji asked from the door.

"Oh, no," I replied, "I have a fear of heights, and we are really up here in the sky."

He immediately looked concerned.

"If you will feel better, I'll close the curtains."

I couldn't let him do that and spoil that incredible view, so I told him it would be fine, that I was all right if I looked straight out, but looking down upset me and so I wouldn't do that.

He motioned me to a chair at a small table by the window and sat opposite me.

"Is there anything you'd like to talk about first? Any questions you have, Patti?"

I really didn't have any, to speak of, so I thought a minute. The only thing that came to my mind was the unusual dream of the night before, which was somewhat revived because of what had occurred at the window a few seconds before. So I repeated my strange dream experience to him, saying that it seemed very out of the ordinary.

As I talked, he listened carefully. It was a thing I would find remarkable time and time again in the future. When anyone was talking, he listened with such total attention, with such courtesy, that it was extraordinary. I was always a bit amazed when people, including me, would prattle on at him and play obvious games because they had his attention. I knew that his attention was so total that the whole gambit had to be transparent to him. However, he knew that this attention was really all that was being sought, and he was wonderfully patient and gracious . . . most of the time.

When I finished my story about the suicide, he laughed softly and waved it off with his hand.

"Oh, that's nothing but a past life resurfacing."

I was speechless. I stared at him. Many old "tapes" from the Roman Catholic influences of my background were running through my head.

"But . . . but," I finally managed, "I thought suicide was a mortal sin . . . that no one recovered from that . . . purgatory or something."

He threw his head back and laughed.

"No, no, Patti, it's simply a mistake like any other mistake—nothing more, nothing less. You pay it off. You keep coming back until you get it right, that's all."

I sat there thinking, having difficulty digesting this astonishing piece of information. So much was running through me so rapidly, I could barely catch it.

I remembered a time in my life when I was in such a state of depression and despair that I seriously considered suicide, seeing no other way out of my pain, and then mysteriously stopping myself just as I was ready to do it.

You simply keep coming back until you get it right.

I thought, too, about my longtime fear of falling. As a child, elevators and rollercoasters terrified me. As an adult, I once stood on top of Hoover Dam and nearly fainted. I could not get on an airplane without being drugged, and even then I always perspired profusely and "held the plane up by the armrests." Every unusual sound the aircraft made sent me into a panic.

As quickly as the memory of all this fear went by me, I realized that this is a way to pay something off. I found myself telling Paulji how I was in airplanes.

He looked at me intently. Then he seemed to come to some decision inside himself.

"You will be completely free of this fear in six months," he said.

After the initiation, the most remarkable part of which was that he left me sitting there in contemplation and went off to a nearby bathroom where I could hear him flushing the toilet and brushing his teeth, I asked him if there was anything I could do for him in the area of service. He told me that he would like me to teach one of the new discussion classes that were beginning to form. I said I would.

But I only said it because he asked me. I felt that I knew so little about ECKANKAR that I was totally unfit to teach a class. But, like everything else I'd done since I'd taken up this path, I knew that not knowing how to do something was the best reason to do it. I painted. I wrote poetry. I read a poem to an audience. Such things had been impossible for me two years before. Of course I would begin a class. But I never did teach it. It taught me.

Four

S hortly after I had agreed to begin teaching a discussion class for him, Paulji said he would send me the names and addresses of all of the chelas in Orange County, California, so I could contact them. Within the week the list arrived. I was surprised to see that there were twenty-four names, enough to begin two classes.

I wrote to the people on the list. Almost everyone responded that they were interested in working with a class. The group broke up nicely into north and south Orange County, my contingent being the southern one.

This first class was a wonderful cross section of society. There were several young housewives besides myself: a painting contractor; several older ladies from a nearby retirement community; an officer from the local Coast Guard station; a nurse; an actress; and a young man, about nineteen years old, with a foot-long ponytail. In those days, one would probably have described him as a hippie.

What a broad spectrum of viewpoint, age, economics, education, and experience! Many of the others were well-read in the esoteric studies, while I, the so-called teacher, had little exposure to these things. I had come almost straight out of Christianity, with a few side-trips reading Edgar Cayce, a few inner or *psi* experiences, and, of course, my dream teachings. Other than that, I knew nothing about the vast wealth of spiritual material out there on the planet, but it was constantly being referred to in Paulji's writings and by one or another individual in the class; so, slowly, I began to learn and widen my horizons.

Since the only other groups in this part of California were the one in north Orange County and another in Los Angeles, the ECK chelas needed some way to communicate. I hit upon the idea of a little newsletter. It was two pages, and I designed a little logo for the front. It was called *Eckos*. It mainly kept track of upcoming seminars and local events, and the chelas often contributed poems or spiritual experiences.

Actually, this was the first ECKANKAR chela newsletter in the world. Apparently Paulji saw a copy of it and thought it was such a good idea that he asked other areas to follow suit. Today, there are many hundreds of these newsletters all over the world and every one of them is much better than *Eckos* was, but it was a seed.

Apparently Paulji saw something else in *Eckos:* there was a potential writer and editor almost in his neighborhood, although at the time I didn't know I was in his vicinity. I thought he lived and worked in Las Vegas. Only later did I discover that he actually lived in the San Diego area about an hour's drive from my home in Newport Beach. Very soon I received word from Helen that Paulji wanted to know if I would help him write and edit the *Mystic World,* a quarterly publication for chelas only.

By now I had learned not to bother with the old insecurity patterns such as, "But I don't know how, I have no training, etc." I trusted Paulji so completely that I knew if he asked me to do something, I could do it. He would never ask an impossible thing of me. He told me later the two pluses I had going for me were that I could learn fast and that I had no previous training; therefore, he did not have to waste a lot of time untraining me.

For months Paulji had been using Helen as a liaison between himself and me. This was almost entirely due to the fact that I was still in what I call my exuberant puppy stage, and he would not abide the undisciplined energy. I was impossible for him to be around for any length of time: my joy and excitement and pure happiness were unbridled. When I had run up to greet him in the lobby the day of my initiation, I had thrown open my arms to give him a spontaneous hug and nearly knocked him down. I was somewhat insensitive.

I was also in such tremendous awe of him that I must have been difficult to deal with.

At the next seminar Paulji set about to cure me of some of this. There was to be a luncheon for a group of people with whom he wanted to go over plans for the Fourth World Wide Seminar, and I was invited. In the restaurant we were seated at a long table; there were approximately fourteen of us. Paulji sat at the end. I had never actually seen him working behind the scenes. Of course, I was going through the usual sensory overload that his presence evoked. My awe and excitement were so great that I simply could not eat one bite of food.

I left the meeting without having touched the food, but promised myself a good supper. At suppertime I was seated with friends, getting ready to order, when who should walk into the coffee shop and sit down at our table but Paulji. My stomach again rebelled at the idea of food, so I quietly ordered a cup of tea. It seemed he was not through with me yet.

In the next two days every single time I sat down to eat, he appeared *by coincidence*. He always chose to sit at my table, and was most friendly and casual, but after about five missed meals in two days I was getting weak. By the evening of the second day, I was experiencing dizziness and looking very pale. I was afraid to sneak down to the coffee shop in between meals because I was sure he'd find me; and stuck alone with him, he'd notice my affliction. At least in a group I didn't stand out. If he knew consciously what he was doing to me, it never showed, but it was obvious that so many mealtime meetings could not be happenstance.

Finally, at suppertime of my second day without food, one of my companions, who was a doctor, said, "Patti, you must eat; you need the nutrition." I looked over at Paulji, who seemed to be oblivious to my presence and my predicament, and at the person's plate next to mine, heaped high with food. I felt the agony in my poor, abandoned stomach and gave it up: I ordered a huge meal, which I ate. Then I cleaned up my neighbor's leftovers. Paulji had literally starved me out. From that day on, I could eat with him and often did.

This was part of the conditioning he put me through so that I would drop all the emotional—what ECKists call, astral—heaviness and be light and easy for him to be around. On my own behalf, I couldn't help the natural outpouring of joy and devotion. In any other chela it would have been understood and tolerated, because it probably would not come up that often. But in me, it was not permissible, because he was getting ready to work with me, personally, on a one-to-one basis. He had to get me calmed down and regulated or I'd be useless to him, too much of a drain on his energy.

Down through the years I have seen many chelas go through this intense nervousness, joy, awe, etc., when in the presence of the Living ECK Master, and I always grin and am filled with good-natured compassion as I remember with mixed emotions the funny-awful experiences of my own puppyhood. It is such a tribute to the Master on the one hand; it says much about the ideals of the chela in question, and it's wonderful—all that love. But in large doses it's difficult to be around for any length of time.

I had an appointment at this seminar to see Paulji at his request. When I arrived, he had spread before him on a table a bunch of blank sheets of paper with vertical lines drawn down them in the familiar, felt-tip black ink.

"This is a dummy," he said.

I hadn't the faintest idea what he was talking about. But patiently he explained that it was a plan for the layout of the *Mystic World*.

"I am going to give you all the articles that I want to go in this issue. Your job will be to figure out a layout and make a plot like this, numbering the stories and pictures. Then we'll turn it over to the printer, and he'll do the rest."

He then spent about thirty minutes showing me how to work with the dummy.

Later when I began dealing directly with him, the printer told me that Paulji would often walk into his shop, dump a basketful of copy and pictures on his desk, and he, the printer, would do the entire dummy, layout, etc. When one reviews some of those old *Mystic Worlds,* it definitely shows.

I had often wondered why there were so many mistakes in that publication. Frequently, a story designated to be continued on a certain page wasn't there; it might be on a different page, under a wrong headline. A story sometimes stopped mid-sentence and that was that. Often the names under the pictures were wrong. It really wasn't the printer's fault; he was trained to follow a dummy, not create one. Because this nice printer couldn't say no to Paul Twitchell, he ended up doing a job he didn't know how to do, about people and a subject he didn't understand. And he probably didn't really have the time or the desire to learn any of it.

Paulji stretched out in his chair for a moment and relaxed.

"You have no idea," he said, "how much help it will be to me if you can learn how to take care of this publication for me. I have so many books to get out, and I need the time to spend on them. Besides this publication I am also writing and publishing the *ECK Monthly Letter*. I am writing the monthly discourses, and I'm only two weeks ahead of the mailing from the office. In addition, I have three new books in some stage of completion. It will be a great service to me," he sighed.

He gave a deadline by which he wanted to have this dummy finished. When I was ready, I should come down to his office with Helen, and he'd go over it with me. I was thrilled with this assignment and, clutching it to my bosom, I thanked him and started to leave.

"Patti," he said, stopping me.

"Yes, sir?"

"I've noticed you have an excellent sense of humor. If you wouldn't mind, I would like you to be one of the speakers at the Fourth World Wide Seminar in October. I'd like you to do a talk that is light and up. People need to laugh. Sometimes this subject of ECK can become very heavy and tiring."

Maybe I said yes, maybe I nodded, I don't remember. I only remember feeling the old panic. The talk he wanted me to give would be in the main showroom at the Stardust Hotel in Las Vegas. My word, I thought, he is really putting the steam to me. A big showroom in Las Vegas. Me. That's a tough one. Blessedly, I didn't know then how very tough it was going to be.

Five

As I think about all that transpired in my time with Paulji, it is difficult to believe that every single bit of it, from the period of my dream teachings until his death, took place in only three and a half years. In those three and a half years I grew so fast, produced so much work, and experienced so much, that it could easily have been a lifetime. This intense concentration of growth and work was necessary because time was running out for him, and he had much left to do.

At the time, I considered it the greatest honor of my life to be able, in some small way, to ease the burden of this incredible human being. Perhaps it is possible that, because he allowed me to carry a small part of the load for him, he could give to the world a little more than he would otherwise have been able to. At least in my quiet times I liked to think that was true and, somehow, because of it, I found the inner resources to shoulder a workload that was staggering, while also looking after a husband and four growing children.

I now feel, so many years later, that in spite of often feeling pushed and stretched far beyond myself, I came here to do exactly what I did. This reflects back to the Knowing I had several years earlier concerning the dream teachings about writing a book. Remember, I said that I knew something important was going to happen, sometime, and once it did, I would write. I have become convinced that this ECKANKAR experience is what that referred to. I had an agreement with this being, whose spiritual name is Peddar Zaskq, and although I still do not have a conscious recall of it, it is there, inside of me as a Knowing — a knowing which is backed up by history. In many respects, the matter really involved a contract to serve, and most of the time I have marched through this drama, not as an officer surveying a large battle-field, but as a common soldier in the trenches on the front line.

Did I cause it to be this way in that elevator? Or is it the lot of all soldiers to march and do their jobs without knowledge of the parleys and processes of the great decision-makers, including, for the most part, themselves prior to the present incarnation? Whatever the truth of it is, no matter what I have done, or how often I might have appeared to be in a role of leadership, I have never been anything but a soldier in the trenches. Nor have I lost the sense of wonder, the sense of the miracle, that all this happened to me, a basically average, unremarkable human being.

For days I worked on my first dummy for the *Mystic World*. It was a long and tedious job because I didn't know how to count words or lines or judge space. I did it the hard way but it worked well, for I had turned the problem over to Spirit. The best part was that once I got the hang of it, all seemed to fall together. The stories blended well. They seemed to know where they went in the dummy, and everything fit exactly. I was ecstatic. I was also dashing headlong into a big, unattractive ego trip.

Another letter arrived from Helen. It said that Paul was going to be in Los Angeles in mid-March, and if it could be worked out, he wanted to give me the Third Initiation. Well, well, well, I thought, I must really be someone important. I only had my Second Initiation two months ago, and here I am about to get number three. No doubt about it, I am a lot more special than I think I am.

One day I was walking through my house, thinking about how some people have so much trouble getting their Master-Chela relationship together. For some, it seems to be a fearful, testing, or suspicious matter. They lack the trust and the understanding that if they would give up everything, they would get it all, and much, much more, back in return. I could see it so clearly, I felt sure I could clear this up for those who were having difficulty.

Immediately I sat down and wrote out a script that I thought would be a wonderful way to confront this issue in a seminar and help everyone. I called it something like: "The Master-Chela Encounter in One Act." I can barely recall it, probably because the memory is still pretty painful, but it was a sort of a play in which the chela confronted, head-on, all these silly fears and doubts. Of course, I had entirely forgotten my own experience of the first year. Feeling sure I had solved this spiritual problem for everyone for all time, I fired the little goodie off to Paulji. Things were certainly going wonderfully. I had put together perfectly my first *Mystic World*, had earned another initiation in three months, and had solved for Paulji the basic dilemma facing almost every new chela.

Not long afterwards I got a letter from Paulji. It seemed that he would not be coming to Los Angeles in March after all, and so I would not be getting the Third Initiation. Perhaps he would give it at the June seminar, if I was ready. It was a thirty-ton boulder which drifted down on me like a feather, it was so polite — until the full weight of it hit me.

If I hadn't wanted or been able to face it, I could have pretended to myself that the letter meant exactly what it said. But I knew, with every fiber of my being, that I had blown it. I knew that I had begun to think that I was someone special. Ego had gotten its hands around my throat and nearly choked me to death. Suddenly, I was so ashamed of myself, I wished I could crawl in a hole somewhere and pull it in

66

after me — terribly embarrassing.

I didn't know what to do or how to handle it. The extent of my error was so vast in my own mind that I couldn't cope with it, which was probably better. I let it go. I said to myself, I don't care if I ever get another initiation. I only want to be able to do my job, and it would be enough if I could serve Paulji well. I don't care if I am a Second Initiate for thirty-five years.

I meant it too. The worst thing that could happen to me, as I saw it, would be if Paulji found me too defective to work with. Obviously, that didn't happen, but I would never make *that* mistake again. And ever after, the initiations, which he took me through with unbelievable speed, never fazed me, nor have I ever really identified myself with them. They are something that takes place "over there," and I, Patti, am over here, just being me.

When I had sufficiently recovered from my ego trip, Paulji sent for me. Helen was to pick me up and bring me to his office. I was to bring my dummy for the *Mystic World*.

Now, this was excitement. I had not blown my job — only an initiation, which I had not dreamed of getting anyway. He must have forgiven me, because he was going to allow me to come to his place. Ah well, folks, it was still puppyland.

Helen drove and drove and drove. I couldn't believe how far south we went. We were in Imperial Beach, and could stand on the street in back of his house and look across the border out to the big bullfight ring by the sea, on the outer edge of Tijuana, Mexico. It was a very desolate, isolated area. But it had those special, magic Paulji vibrations that never failed to raise the hair on my arms and put Soul into the hyperalert state. Later, as I made many of these trips on my own, I discovered that Paulji had a certain area surrounding his home base in which I could feel his vibrations. It radiated out about a mile from his home and followed him to his new home when he moved. I never thought about it until it suddenly encompassed me on the freeway, a certain distance from his home.

The setup he had in Imperial Beach was interesting. He and Gail lived in an apartment building that fronted on the ocean. Upstairs, overlooking the water, were their living quarters. In the same building, but back about three units and overlooking the street in back, was Paulji's office. Both his office and his living quarters were up a flight of stairs.

I was really jumpy and jittery. As we walked up the stairs to his office, I noticed someone's throw rug hanging over a balcony. How really ordinary! It's hard to believe this man is working here among all these plain, normal everyday people.

Helen knocked on Paulji's office door. He opened it and ushered us into a two-bedroom apartment that was stripped for action. There were desks and typewriters in both bedrooms as well as in the living room, which was the main office. Boxes of Paul Twitchell books were all over the kitchen. In the center of the living room was a blue desk, and off to one side, in the dining area, was a large table with all sorts of papers on it. It was to this table that he beckoned me for our first official work session.

Now was my moment. I had blown it on the initiation, but I knew that this *Mystic World* was perfect. I had tried it every way imaginable and it was right. I was very proud of my first effort and anxious for him to see it. Perhaps it would get me back in his good graces. I handed him the dummy with a huge grin on my face, then sat back and watched with delight while he studied it. He looked through it quickly, turning each page, and after that, he went back to page one. He then took out the famous felt-tipped pen and began to scratch all over it.

"This won't do! It doesn't belong on the front page."

Slash, slash, slash went the pen as one after another of my perfect pages fell under his critical eye. In the end it appeared he hadn't liked any of it, although I knew it was far, far better than anything the printer had done. I could feel my spirits plummeting into the depths with each slash of his pen, and my head was beginning to pound.

"I'd like you to take this into that front bedroom," he said, "and work on it. See if you can fix it while Helen and I go over our business out here."

Broken, I marched into the front bedroom with my mutilated dummy and a throbbing headache. What could I do with it? I honestly had given my very best. How could I now give any more? Why was he doing this to me?

I wandered around the room, feeling a little like a banished child, and looked the place over: desk, a typewriter, and above the typewriter, taped to the wall, was the chapter outline to the book he had going on that particular machine. In each room, at each typewriter, was another book working and another outline on the wall above it. He was always writing three books simultaneously.

I put the dummy down on the desk and tried to look at it. My head was hurting so much I couldn't stand to read it, much less think about it, and try to "redo perfection." So, I wandered about the room. I read the chapter outline above the typewriter. As I recall it was *Herbs: The Magic Healers*. Then I saw another paper taped on the wall to the right. I walked over to see what it was. I got as far as the title and then thought I would surely die. It was entitled, "The Master-Chela Encounter in One Act," and was written by you-know-who. At this point, I actually became nauseous.

Back to puppyland. I had certainly gotten my nose wiped in it. My ego was a withered, all but invisible remnant, and it did seem to me that he was into overkill. Nevertheless, I'd been sent into this Siberia (it was also freezing cold in that room) to do a task, and I'd best get on with it.

I picked up the perfect dummy and looked it over for possible revisions. Someone was pounding on my head with a ballpeen hammer. I was shivering in the cold, miserable beyond measure,

70

and soon knew one thing: There was no way, in my present condition, that I could redo that dummy. I would tell Paulji that and ask him to let me take it back home and work some more on it.

It seemed like forever before he called me out of my prison. I didn't know him well enough to understand that he was arranging and manipulating this whole thing.

I told him, miserably, about my terrible headache and my inability to redo the dummy. I asked if I could try it at home, and he said sure. I made no mention of what I had seen on the wall in there, and it was never spoken of between us, ever. I knew what it was there for. I got the message. That was all that mattered.

"Now, if you have the time," he said cheerfully, "I'm going to take you two lovely ladies out to lunch."

Helen was delighted. I was so miserable and ill that the idea of spending another ten minutes with him was difficult to bear, but I didn't know how to get out of it.

We got into Helen's car. Helen drove, Paulji sat in the front seat beside her, and I huddled in my fur coat in the back seat, cold, my head banging like a jungle drum, and my whole microcosm in a state of acute trauma. I stared morosely at the back of his head, which was, as usual, crowned by a jaunty, navy blue Greek fisherman's cap.

Paulji, by this time, was in the jolliest of moods. I guess he could see that he had really gotten to me.

"Well, Miss Patti, tell me what you know about the printing profession," he said, without turning his head.

I shoved my hands deeper into my coat pockets and mumbled.

"What did you say?" he asked.

"Nothing," I said dejectedly, "I know nothing about the printing profession."

"That's the right answer," he said. I could swear he was choking back laughter.

I don't remember much more about that day, except that once again I sat at the table with the great man, and once again was unable to eat my lunch. However, I was rapidly making the transition from eager, affectionate puppy to soldier in the trenches.

So much for the glamorous aspects of my new job.

Six

In the weeks that followed my disastrous visit to his house, Paulji helped me get the *Mystic World* dummy straightened out. Witholding all personal observations, I redid the thing. However, my changes were minor and I was neutral about them. I honestly didn't care whether the dummy came out perfectly or not and returned it to him in the mail. When the final product emerged, I noticed that he had changed most of my new layout back to the way I had originally done it. I permitted myself a small giggle, but it was no more than mild amusement. To have registered any sort of glee or self-satisfaction would have been like grabbing onto the ubiquitous, octopus-like tentacles of the ego trap which dangle about us at all times. While I would fight this trap on other occasions, in new circumstances and roles, never again would it snare me in the layout business.

Because of Paulji, I have pretty much eliminated this kind of pride from my repertoire, but there is one area of my experience about which I remain proud. That is, to my knowledge, I have never made the same mistake twice. Actually, that is not really such a remarkable feat, considering how many mistakes are available to us without our needing to repeat any. And I say, with some chagrin, that while I may not hold the record, I have accomplished a respectable volume of work in that category.

Paulji didn't see mistakes as fatal but considered them in the vein of the popular saying, "A mistake is a sign that someone tried to do something." I know of people who are almost paralyzed because they are afraid to make a mistake, and so they find it difficult to be "cause" and have experiences, or to follow their inner voice. I used to be like that, so I understand, but Paulji taught me to think for myself and to be courageous. Eventually I dropped that old fearful self and began to operate from the viewpoint that it is usually easier to get forgiveness than permission.

But the clock was ticking away. I had to be up to speed and fast. Paulji demanded that I learn to be cause, to trust myself and my instincts, and this meant very rapidly overcoming a lifetime of fears, insecurities, and a sense of inadequacy.

Right now, on the wall in my workroom is a framed cartoon which he once mailed to me during the time he was teaching me to be cause without fear. It is a cartoon cut from a magazine which depicts a bird, wearing a parachute, huddled on a tree branch. Another bird stands beside him, saying in the caption: "The trouble with you, Sheldon, is you lack self-confidence." I no longer lack self-confidence, but I keep the cartoon on my wall anyway as a reminder; because there are times when life deals a difficult hand — such as when something that seems so right comes from my inner guide but is rejected — and I begin to forget my friend's lessons. When I start to feel my confidence slipping and begin to revert back into old patterns, I walk over and look at old Sheldon huddled there with his parachute, and I gain new resolve.

This subject of the rejection of one's inner guidance is a tender one, and one that is often difficult for us to understand. What *is* the inner guidance, or voice, anyway? And how come mine led me to Paul Twitchell and another man's led him to try to harm him? What is the difference between someone who follows guidance that comes from the highest in himself, and someone else who hears voices and is locked away in an insane asylum? I think it's time to introduce the bus.

Several years ago, after the death of my husband, I went to Tahiti for a much needed vacation. On the island of Bora Bora, I met and became friends with Jim, a young attorney from, of all places, San Diego, California. He was wonderful company as he had a great sense of humor and made me laugh a lot, which was what I desperately needed to do at that time of my life.

We were both guests of a private club and met every mealtime at community tables, much as one would on a cruise ship. Each morning at breakfast, Jim and I would sit together and he would regale me with tales of his romantic misadventures of the previous evening. He was always trying to find a beautiful woman to have one of those storybook tropical flings with, but somehow he always ended up sabotaging himself and striking out.

One morning he arrived at the table looking particularly rough around the edges. Anticipating a really good story, I inquired as to how his evening had gone. He rolled his eyes and sighed. "You wouldn't believe it," he said.

"Try me," I laughed.

"Well," he said, "in order to understand what happened, I have to introduce you to my bus. You see, I am not really one individual. I am a busload of individuals, and who I am and what I do depends largely upon who is driving my bus at any given moment."

I was really intrigued.

"For example," he went on, "a few months ago I left my steady girlfriend to go skiing in Aspen, Colorado, for a weekend. However, I have this character in my bus I call 'The Midnight Rider.' When he starts driving, anything can happen.

"I got to Aspen for a weekend of skiing and suddenly the Midnight Rider began driving the bus. I didn't come home for two weeks. By then, my girlfriend was no longer my girlfriend. Now, I, myself, didn't have the courage to break up with her, which I knew had to be done, but the Midnight Rider fixed it."

Knowing I was in for a really good story, I prodded him on about last night's adventure.

"Last night," he said, "I met the most beautiful creature I have ever seen. She was gorgeous, and she liked me. We danced several dances and I could tell that something good was going to come of this.

"I asked if she'd like a drink and she said yes, so we went to the bar and I ordered one for each of us. While we stood there waiting, an Australian fellow next to me struck up a conversation, in the course of which he mentioned the drinking prowess of the Australians. The American didn't live, he said, who could hold a candle to any Australian in this arena."

At this point Jim's eyes grew large and a knowing smile spread across his face.

"You have to understand, Patti. I had this gorgeous girl with me, and I was planning a lovely evening for the two of us. I wasn't going to go for his challenge. No way! But this Australian had thrown down the gauntlet, and before I even knew what was happening, the Midnight Rider had slipped in and said, 'I can handle this one,' and he was in the driver's seat. The rest is history. Many drinks later, I turned to look for the pretty girl, but she was gone. To multiply my woes, I also lost the contest."

When I returned home from Tahiti, I often thought about Jim and his bus. He had hit upon a profound truth — that is, we are, each of us, a bus-load of people, not just one person. It is another way of describing what Paulji called the microcosm — the miniature, personal replica of the macrocosm. Paulji said that whatever is "out there" is also "in here." No matter what it is, person, place, or thing, mood, personality, saint, or sinner, we have all those possibilities inside us . . . or, as I find it easier to think of now, inside our bus. Therefore, we will be whoever is driving the bus. Being "cause" means we ourselves make the conscious decision about who drives the bus at any given moment. Or, if we are just flowing with the moment, we may allow the spontaneous driver to take over, but again, watchfully, and with conscious agreement.

Jim knew who the Midnight Rider was, and, in spite of his protests to the contrary, he turned his bus over to him quite deliberately and with gusto. However, had he been unaware of the bus and the Midnight Rider, his behavior could have been rather compulsive and reactive.

To get back to the question: Why are some inner voices beneficial to ourselves and to others, and some very destructive and crazy? It is simply a matter of who is driving the bus. If Soul or the Inner Master is driving the bus, then what might *seem* crazy, such as my ten canvases, turns out not to be at all. However, how one determines this is a complex subject.

I've found a good rule of thumb, a test that Paulji suggested. Before taking any actions we are not sure of, we ask ourselves three questions: Is it true? Is it necessary? Is it kind? Each individual's physical, mental, emotional, psychic, and spiritual space is his own. It is a violation of spiritual law to intrude upon another's space without his permission. Therefore, if our inner guidance leads us to violate this law, or if we cannot answer yes to all three questions, we are on shaky ground.

Students of ECKANKAR often ask me questions like, "How can I overcome the negativity that keeps sneaking in?" "How do you turn it over to the Master or Spirit?" In other words, how does one get control over one's personal universe?

Once they understand the concept of the bus, and that all their role models, ideals, or states are within the bus, I have them go back inside their bus and find the personification of that which they desire to be, and then put that personification in the driver's seat.

This is exactly what I did at my first seminar when I had to read the poem and couldn't. There is a Paulji in my bus—and I put him in the driver's seat.

Paulji was teaching me to put a Patti I had never even met, except once in a dream, in the driver's seat of my bus, and to put good old Sheldon and his parachute in the back somewhere. The key was to eliminate the habit of assigning value judgments and conditioned responses to everything. In order for Paulji to work with me as he needed to, I had to be non-reactive and non-judgmental, or in a word, neutral. I had to learn to operate from my highest self at all times when dealing with him. Sometimes our interaction was not in the form of obvious work, but took the form of gentle jokes, funny stories, or swapping plant cuttings from our gardens. No matter what we did, I had to learn to do it with the lightness of my child-self and with no motive but the sharing of the thing itself in the moment.

The experiences he put me through in order to round off the hard edges would seem rather strange to some folks. Perhaps some of the experiences seem almost cruel, but I never looked at them in that way. I understood that he had to get me shaped up. If, at times, it seemed he'd been exceptionally rough or unfair (a term I ceased using very soon), I would remember the hardships that an adept named Milarepa was put through by his own master.

For those not familiar with Milarepa's dilemma, his master pointed to a spot and told him to build a stone house. Milarepa did this, hauling stones up the mountain. It was exhausting work, but finally he finished and awaited his master's approval. But the master, when he saw it, frowned and said, "This is not a good place, move the house over here," and he pointed out a new spot. Milarepa then had to tear the new house down stone by stone and rebuild it on the new spot. I don't recall how many times he had to move it, but at least once more. Why was this necessary?

Milarepa had been headstrong in the past. He'd

achieved great states of awareness but then abused his powers and created trouble which had resulted in many deaths. The moving of the house was his master's way of testing him for impatience, anger, vanity—all of the areas he had not perfected the first time. Compared to Milarepa's discipline, I felt I was getting off pretty easily.

Paulji, however, was like the Chinese Water Torture in moderating my strong opinions.

Once my husband had ordered me a new car. I selected the color by merely looking at a small color swatch. The shade I picked out was a light green. Later, he pointed the color out to me on a whole car. It was positively nauseating—a bilious, metallic pea-soup green—and I instantly hated it.

Weeks went by and my car, which was being built in Michigan and shipped to California by rail, didn't materialize. Weeks stretched into months, and finally, wondering what was holding up the delivery, I mentioned it to my husband.

"Oh, I guess I forgot to tell you," he said, "the train carrying the shipment with your car got in a wreck in New Mexico, and your new car was totaled. I ordered you another one. Since you hated that color, I ordered yellow."

I didn't say anything, but I thought what a fortuitous train wreck.

One day, Paulji had called me about something and I told him the story of the hated green car and the train wreck in New Mexico. There was a silence on the other end of the line for awhile.

"You've got quite a few of those things out there, don't you?" he said quietly.

Up until that moment, I had viewed the whole thing as rather humorous and had not seriously considered the possibility that I could have had any responsibility for the train wreck. Perhaps I did, perhaps I didn't; I'll never know for sure. But I did realize that he was telling me something important about my thought forms, and I began a rigorous self-examination to see just how many of "those things" I did have out there. I truly did not know. But I tried very hard to curb that sort of strong opinion in the future.

I realize that some readers would probably find it difficult to understand why one needs to drop opinions. That would seem to be some form of brainwashing or conditioning, creating a sort of robotlike being. Actually, it's the opposite. The strong likes and dislikes and fixed opinions we hold *are* the conditioning and the brainwashing of the outer world, society, parents, teachers, friends, and, in some cases, the karma brought over from other lives.

Upon dropping these strong opinions, one does not become a robot, incapable of discrimination, thought, and decision making — although that sometimes is a temporary problem while one is in the actual process of learning to function in the freer state. When we are in the neutral zone, we are much closer to ourselves as Soul. We are in the state of being truly open-minded and no longer have problems when our plans don't go our way. If we are forced to change directions, it is no big deal. There is not a huge emotional investment, so there is not a lot to unwind before we are able to change. This allows us the freedom to flow and move and change and to remain balanced and unbothered while we are doing so. It is a great task to learn to do this and still be an effective member of society, a success in business and relationships, but it can be done. It is being done, but it is very difficult.

All through this memoir there will be anecdotes in which we see Paulji reworking my viewpoints, opinions, and mindsets. The world tells us we must have these things to exist and function intelligently, but it is not so. Each one we hold is like a colored lens placed over our true vision and everything we look at is viewed through this lens. The more opinions and mindsets we have, the more colored and complex is the lens through which we view and react to our world. If someone had looked at my lens when I first began to study ECKANKAR, they would have seen a stained glass window to rival any in the Cathedral of Notre Dame.

Except for rare occasions, the only way to get back our clear vision is to remove the bits of glass from our lenses, color by color. But on the other hand, we are each given golden moments when our lenses are mysteriously removed and we see clearly.

The free and independent Patti I experienced in

the beauty spa dream had no colored glass over her vision, and her discrimination was impeccable. I wanted very much to get back to being her. It seems ironic that some of us spend a lifetime filling ourselves with education, information, and sophistication, developing a viewpoint that distinguishes us with those we wish to be respected by, only to decide we have a spiritual goal which dictates that we change all of our attitudes as they apply to these things.

In June of that year, 1970, five months after I had received my Second Initiation, Paulji attended the regional seminar in Sherman Oaks, California. I had an appointment to see him for my Third Initiation, about which I was only semi-excited since I was now practicing the neutral way.

At the appointed time I knocked on his door, carrying a beautiful, big orange in my hand, as it is the ECK custom for the candidate for initiation to present the initiator with a gift of fruit as a symbolic gesture of giving one's self to God.

Right before the seminar I had returned with my husband from a weekend trip to San Francisco. We had traveled by airplane and I experienced none of the old fear of heights, just as Paulji had promised. This was the first thing I wanted to share with him. Imagine, only six months ago I was a Second Initiate and terrified of heights. Here I was, about to become a Third, and this fear was gone.

I sat down before him. He looked thoughtful and had the far-off, dreamy kind of look I would learn to know so well, a look that made his eyes seem like a vast seashore; while he, himself, seemed to be watching an expansive vision going on somewhere else. When he did this, his eyes were always wide open, but rather out of focus.

"I've been thinking about this, Patti, and I think, if you are agreeable, we will give you the Fifth Initiation today."

"The Fifth!" I yelled and jumped up, staring at him in disbelief. Oh dear. So much for neutral.

I began to pace the room, actually I was going around in circles, trying to get hold of myself. The Fifth Initiation was the initiation of the Mahdis level, or the equivalent of a minister or priest. Today an ECK student will study for approximately fourteen years before attaining this level of initiation. In the early times of ECKANKAR, Paulji cut the times of these initiations for a lot of people because he needed the leaders. Of all those who were given accelerated initiations, however, only a handful of us remain. And among those of us who were accelerated, I imagined that he poured it to me the fastest of all.

He could see that I was really upended by this surprise.

"If you don't feel that you can handle the Fifth at this time," he said kindly, "we can postpone it and go ahead with the Third."

Now I had a decision to make; it wasn't a difficult one. It was made the way I approached everything these days. Who would I trust?

Myself, who was in a state of shock and insecurity? or him, who I knew would not suggest this to me if I couldn't handle it?

I grinned at him. "I trust you, Paulji," I said. "If you say I can do it, I know I can."

He smiled back and said quietly, "You can do it."

As I prepared to leave, following my entry into the Fifth Circle, he halted me.

"By the way, now that you're a new Fifth Initiate, I have another job for you. As of now, you are also doing the *ECK Monthly Letter*.

And so I entered the level of the High Initiate. For most people this is a tremendous rite of passage. It was definitely special for me too. However, my greatest rite of passage was dealing with this unique man right at the vortex of his life's work.

I made some interesting entries about the Sherman Oaks Seminar in a journal I kept sporadically during my days with Paulji. The following is from that journal:

> It seemed there in Sherman Oaks that Paulji was everywhere in the hotel. Chelas were astounded to step into an elevator and find a smiling Paulji standing there. He took all of his meals in the hotel coffee shop and invited as many chelas to join him at his table as it would accommodate.
>
> After his lectures he remained in the hallways to shake hands and speak with all who wished to meet him. Paulji seemed to be

enjoying himself hugely.

There were many incidents that occurred in the Sherman Oaks Lectures that will delight future collectors of Pauljibilia. One that was observed by about a dozen people involved the sluggish elevator system of that particular hotel. There were delays in elevator service of up to five minutes from the time the button was pushed until an elevator arrived.

One afternoon, Paulji and the above mentioned dozen chelas stood waiting for an exceptionally long time. One of the High Initiates began to get uneasy that the Living ECK Master was being slowed down by a recalcitrant elevator. With great finesse, the initiate commandeered a service elevator, obtaining permission from the elevator operator to take this very important personage upstairs to his room.

All the chelas crowded in first, calling to Paulji to come aboard. He waited until they were all in it, then smiled and said, "No, thank you." With that he turned and it looked as if he were going to walk straight into a closed elevator door, which suddenly opened for him, and he sauntered in with no facial expression, seemingly oblivious to the whole comical scene as the doors closed on his loyal followers in the elevator that had been obtained for him, while he rode to his floor in solitary, and, no doubt, blessed silence.

I have already mentioned the business meeting at a previous seminar during which I was unable to eat. The color of that lens is: *Great spiritual happenings cannot coexist with mundane activities.*

There was an occurrence at another luncheon meeting which gives a good insight into the way Paulji functioned.

There were approximately twelve to fourteen of us seated at a long table, and Paulji was at the head of it with his back to the service area and kitchen door. He was speaking to the attentive gathering, and all eyes were fastened on him. As he spoke, the kitchen door opened and a young man wheeled out a stack of wire racks about eight feet tall, all filled with freshly washed cups and glasses.

Since this was going on directly behind Paulji, and all of us were looking at him, we all watched in fascination as the young man got to a place about three feet behind Paulji, where his load began to teeter. I let out a loud gasp and Paulji's words were drowned out by the crash and clatter of breaking glass as hundreds of cups and glasses hit the floor. A waitress nearby was struck on the back of the leg by one of the falling racks, but miraculously there were no injuries.

Paulji turned for an instant to see what had interrupted him, then turned back to the table with barely a two-second interval and continued his sentence right where he had left off, as unaffected by the incident as if he had merely brushed a fly from his face.

It was nearly impossible to hear the rest of his talk due to the clatter made by those cleaning up all the broken glass.

As I watched this, I was thinking that this sort of disturbance must be a common occurrence in his life. He honestly didn't seem to notice.

Another incident took place in Sherman Oaks that details yet another aspect of this extraordinary individual. A certain man, not a student of Paulji's, had heard much about Paulji as an unusual and gifted Master. A friend had invited him to attend Paulji's lectures, and later this man told this story which I recorded in my journal:

> A most unusual thing happened. As I was driving up for the lecture, I was thinking about Paul Twitchell and wondering what he would be like. It came to me that he would be about five foot eight and weigh 165 pounds.
>
> "When his lecture was over, I went down to the coffee shop for a snack, and who should I find myself standing right next to but Paul himself. He was having a late supper, it seemed, and after a short exchange, he invited me to join him at his table.
>
> "During the dinner I got to thinking back to my thoughts in the car on the way up there and decided to check them out. I asked, 'How tall are you, Paul?' and he said, 'Five foot eight.' Then I asked, 'How much do you weigh?' and he replied, '165 pounds.'
>
> "It is the most fantastic experience I can remember. I had all that information before I ever saw him."

The gentleman never did know what a fantastic experience he really had, for Paul Twitchell was *not* five foot eight and did not weigh 165 pounds. He was closer to five foot six and weighed probably 150 pounds. The gentleman, without his knowledge, had been treated to one of the rare experiences of having an ECK Master speaking directly into his consciousness and telling him exactly what he most needed to hear at that particular moment in his life.

The whole seminar experience in Sherman Oaks was a good one. However, with the new assignment and the unexpected Fifth Initiation, I had had my share of surprises. I returned home, barely able to realize all that had happened to me.

The afternoon I arrived home, I walked to a bench in my patio and sat down. I closed my eyes to relax and sort it all out. To my delight and amazement, a new thing was now going on inside me. With my eyes closed, I was no longer looking at the inside of my eyelids, but out into a beautiful, starry night. The sky overhead was a vast dome. I could even feel the temperature there, some degrees cooler than my sun-drenched yard. What I was looking at had both temperature and dimension, exactly like looking through an open window into another room, albeit, a vast one. What in the world was going on now? I could not remember coming across this in any of Paulji's writings, just as I had not come upon anything that explained what had been going on in my twenty-one nights of dream teachings.

I sat there, looking into this starry night, feeling its peace and coolness. I opened my eyes. There was my elm tree, my Japanese garden, the arbor of redwood, and the hot sun. Eyes closed, there was again the starry night! I went back and forth like this for awhile, testing to see if this new thing was a fluke that would disappear, but it stayed with me.

I found this inner world that appeared to me whenever I closed my eyes to be restful, and I never tired of it. If I had to wait at the dentist's office, I was not bored or restless; I merely closed my eyes and looked into this wonderful world. Now, it seemed that I had been given a special gift, something that would give instant peace and forever eradicate impatience and boredom from my waking hours. This must be what it's like to be a High Initiate, I thought. Funny, no one ever mentioned this aspect. With reason. It was all over in three days. I was learning rapidly that with this ECKANKAR, you may as well not get attached to your great experiences, because they are usually transitory. One had best enjoy what one had in the moment, for it could be gone in the next.

Seven

The summer of 1970 was full of work and plans. I was working on the publications, sending the dummies and layout materials down to Paulji, and he would see to the printing of them. The local chelas were planning a big picnic for September, and my Satsang class was going well.

In July, the first chapter of *The Shariyat-Ki-Sugmad,* Book One, arrived in the mail. It often happened that Paulji, in order to raise enough funds to keep the fledgling organization afloat, would sell a book-in-progress by the chapter. It also often happened that he was barely a chapter ahead of the mailing. I think, in some ways, this not only provided badly needed revenue, but also was a good incentive for him to keep himself at the typewriter.

Of all of the books he had written and was writing, *The Shariyat-Ki-Sugmad* was the most exciting for many of us. As Paulji explained it, this would be the scriptural texts of ECKANKAR. This first volume would be, as near as is possible with language, the information that is kept in one of what the ECK Masters call the Temples of Golden Wisdom. The temple that has the original, unabridged version of Book One is an inaccessible monastery in northern Tibet. There are twelve main temples in all: three in the physical world and the rest in the inner worlds. The ECK teachings say that the Living ECK Master or one of the other Masters of the Order of Vairagi, which is the ECK line of teaching masters, will often take spiritual students out of their bodies in the dream state to one of these temples to study the ancient wisdom. Now Paulji was putting this esoteric wisdom down in written form.

The day my first chapter arrived in the mail, I rushed to the kitchen table, opened it, and sat down to read. I was only a few paragraphs into it when goose bumps rose all over my arms. A great sense of wonder pervaded me. I knew these words! I couldn't keep reading; it was too much. I jumped up and began pacing the room. So! That's what it had been: the twenty-one nights; my dream teachings of two years before! I sat down and read a few more sentences, then jumped up again and resumed the pacing. The experience was more than I could handle in one sitting. Unable to contain my joy and wonder, I finally wrote down the experience in a kind of poetic essay, which I have saved.

The Shariyat-Ki-Sugmad

Today I began to read
The Shariyat-Ki-Sugmad.
As the words washed over me,
they evoked a vague, almost
aching memory . . . oh yes, I have heard
these words before . . . in some beautiful
time and place . . . but I could not keep
them . . . bring them back to comfort
me . . . strengthen me . . . silence me!

All I could bring back was a remembered
joy . . . a knowing that there is, just
beyond my reach, an all-pervading truth,
and when I see IT, know IT . . . I am
whole . . . without need or
desire . . . enveloped in a blissful
peace . . . a white silence which contains
all things in perfect harmony.

All I could keep was the remembered feel
of it . . . the knowledge of the truths
revealed disappeared as sand trickles
through one's fingers . . . leaving
behind a few grains . . . a memory . . . and a
longing . . . to return.

And now the Godman with this
unfathomable love for all, channels it
down, distills it into thought, which he
then shapes into words . . .
I am barely able to sit and read it, for
my heart jumps, leaps, soars in the
freedom of joyous remembering . . . and once
again, I KNOW.

95

O rare and precious gem!
Miracle taking place before the eyes
of man.
Today . . . I held a piece of heaven in my
hand!

The experience with *The Shariyat-Ki-Sugmad*
proved to me, beyond a shadow of a doubt, that its
volumes do exist; I knew because I had "read"
them. But it also demonstrates how difficult it is
to put the inner experience into words. I have
talked to people who recall going to one of these
Temples of Golden Wisdom and can describe the
edifice. Some saw — actually saw — a book.
Many of them recall the face of, and their experience with, the particular ECK Master who took
them to the temple. And yet, I did not see a Master
of any kind, nor a temple, or a book.

This points up an unfortunate thing about any
written record of the inner realities. One writes as
one experiences. Another reads that experience
and too often gets the notion that this is what he
must experience too. Then, if his own experience
is different, he invalidates it.

Often folks do not realize that this is what they
do, because they have a fixed notion from what
they read that it has to be exactly the way the
writer experienced it. This is a classic example of
why opinions, and the habit of having them, are
often counterproductive for us. The color of this
bit of lens is: *Everyone has to have the identical
experience in order for them to have experienced
the same thing.*

I had my twenty-one nights of experience in a state of dual consciousness, but it was only information running through me. Nevertheless, the minute I began reading *The Shariyat-Ki-Sugmad* in the physical, I knew that was what I had been hearing.

I thought about this for a long time. I must have needed all that information, which was gurgling below my surface, before I could respond to Paul Twitchell's invitation. As Soul, I could process and handle this information, but my mind and the rest of my tools here could not. I had to grow in awareness before I could consciously handle it. Pretty neat how that worked, for I am able, in retrospect, to see how Soul can cognize information that the mind can't even begin to process.

The heart is often a metaphor for what we call Soul, which can know what the mind cannot fathom. One of the pivotal things that Paulji brought out, and insisted that every student learn, is that Soul is the driving, cognizing, energizing, and ongoing eternal spark within each of us. He was very strict on the use of terminology. Once initiated into the works of ECK, one had to eliminate forever from his speech and thought patterns such phrases as "I have a Soul" or "*my*" Soul. One had to make the shift in viewpoint to this: "I *am* Soul. I have a body. I have emotions. I have a mind. But I, the essential being, am Soul. These other facets are merely my tools for experiencing here."

This viewpoint has become such a part of me that now whenever I hear or read the words "my soul" or "I have a soul," a discordant bell rings within me, very much like incorrect English does, or a sour note in a piece of music. Those who are keeping track will have registered a paradox here. The book that changed my life was called, *In My Soul I am Free*. That title was not Paulji's choice for the book. However, I have tried to retitle that book in my own mind, to make it state accurately what it is trying to say, but that is a discourse in itself. Try it, you'll see what I mean.

* * *

Paulji's schedule for the summer of 1970 was very busy. He made a major tour of Europe in May and June, just before the Sherman Oaks seminar at which I got my Fifth Initiation, and in August he was off overseas again. I kept notes on his schedule. It will give a sense of how he pushed himself.

NORWEGIAN SEMINAR
Oslo, Norway, May 17-18

SWEDISH SEMINAR
Stockholm, Sweden, May 20-24

MID-GERMANIC SEMINAR
Stuttgart, Germany, May 25-27

ZURICH SEMINAR
Zurich, Switzerland, May 28-31

BRITISH ISLES SEMINAR
London, England, May 31-June 5

After Sherman Oaks, California:

CONSULTATIONS
Istanbul, Turkey, August 3-5

CONSULTATIONS
Vienna, Austria, August 5-8

CONSULTATIONS
Brussels, Belgium, August 8-10

CONSULTATIONS
Madrid, Spain, August 11-15

CONSULTATIONS
Lisbon, Portugal, August 16-19

CONSULTATIONS
London, England, August 19-24

No doubt, I would not be seeing much of Paulji that summer. When he and Gail left in August, I had all my work laid out for me. He said he would call me in early September. Helen and I were busy on a bunch of art projects, and I was planning the picnic.

Then problems arose. I will quote from my journal an entry in mid-August.

I do not know what troubles me at this time, but I am not up to par physically or mentally . . . this seems to create a spiritual drag too, or is it all the reverse? At any rate, something seems to be draining my energy. I am having a lot of physical problems which, although not terribly serious, are pesky and annoying and demand attention.

I am having some weird dreams these days. I think I am working off karma, and some of it is so violent, and the physical sensations from the dreams so strong, that it carries over to the physical body. I feel lousy after such a night. During the day, I have many negative feelings and tremendous fatigue. Sometimes I have trouble raising my arms above my head to comb my hair.

I had a dream the other night that has unnerved me. Paulji came to me in the dream and seemed normal in every way. We were talking as usual, when inexplicably, he took off his shirt. All over his chest were white spots about two inches in diameter. It looked as if all his blood had gone away there. In all my years working as a nurse, I never saw an affliction like this. It was very upsetting.

Paulji kept on talking to me as if there was nothing unusual about this. He was his regular self.

I could not bring myself to ask him about these white spots. I knew something was wrong but kept pretending that I did not notice. The whole dream was of me trying to avoid facing the truth I was seeing with my own eyes. I refused to think about those spots, and just put them from my mind.

One morning I arose with a very strange inner feeling. It came in the thought: Someone needs me. I didn't know who needed me, but I was extremely restless and uneasy. Who? Who needs me? I found no answer to this question. However, the feeling was pulling so strongly that I decided to get in my car and drive. Perhaps I would get the intuitive, inner punch when I found the one who needed me. I had the feeling it could be anyone, even someone I didn't know. For some reason that I didn't understand then, and don't to this day, I put on a wig, a different color than my hair, and dark glasses. Wherever I was going, it was incognito.

I got in my car and drove down the freeway, headed south. I had a slight twinge when I got to the San Juan Capistrano off ramp, so I turned off there. I saw a coffee shop and pulled in. I ordered a cup of coffee and sat looking around. Would the person who needed me make contact? Would he or she smile at me or strike up a conversation? No one did. I drank my coffee and left.

Further on, around Oceanside I had a repeat of this twinge; but again, nothing. I drove on, thinking that at any time I would get the impulse from a silent cry for help, but it never came. Soon I found myself in San Diego, without the foggiest notion of what to do there. So I drove to a place known as Shelter Island, sat on the grass in my bizarre disguise, and watched the U.S. Navy ships go by. At the time I knew absolutely no one in San Diego except Paulji, but he was in Europe. So I finally gave up my weird odyssey and went home, more puzzled than ever.

Around that time I had another odd dream— almost a nightmare. Someone, whom I couldn't see clearly, came up to me with a huge syringe about a foot long. I was more puzzled than frightened and seemed to feel that this situation was friendly, and that I would not be harmed. The shadowy figure put the syringe into the area of my solar plexus. I didn't feel it go in, but then he began to withdraw something from me, which I did feel. It felt as if some of my energy, or life force, was sucked out into the syringe; I could feel it clear down to the physical body, which immediately felt a surge of nausea. That was all.

What, I wondered, was all that about? The nausea subsided when I awoke, but the memory lingered on. Who is taking away my life force? Is that why I am so tired? It was pretty strange; I had never heard of such a thing. However, the next day I was more tired than ever, looking very pale and hollow-cheeked. I was uneasy, wondering about these odd happenings.

Apparently I went back to my journal and tried to work the thing out by seizing upon some spiritual explanation. One of the colors in my lens was: *Never admit you are tired, weak, or down.* This sounded as if it could be my problem.

> I think what I have been doing is resisting my own fatigue. I have been pushing myself too hard. I have not told anyone of my enervation or my negative feelings which seem to manifest in tears of frustration and a feeling of helplessness.
>
> Now I am admitting all this is true. I am accepting my ebb and am simply not going to expect too much from myself. I think this was the big problem.
>
> All of the Fifth Initiates I know have been having a rough time of it, so there is probably more going on than what we see here. Is this part of our purification, I wonder? Or is the negative force just at us? Oh well, it doesn't matter . . . what is, IS, and there's nothing to be done about it but see it through.

I decided to check up on my health so I made an appointment to see a doctor who had become a special friend, and was also an old friend and chela of Paulji's.

I visited him the last week in August. Paulji would be coming back soon, and there would be a lot of work to do preparing for the World Wide Seminar in October, in Las Vegas. And . . . I had that talk to do. I was going to have to get myself up—and soon.

I didn't tell all of it to the doctor. Mainly, I went into how tired I felt and how odd it was that I didn't recall having been sick. He was very concerned and pumped me for more history. Although I thought it pretty silly, I finally told him about my strange inner experience of the syringe. I said, "I don't understand what was going on there. Do you think there could be some connection?" He said he didn't know.

I believe I also told him about the odd dream in which I saw Paulji with all those white spots on his chest and of my worry that we High Initiates, with our negative experiences, were a drain on him, and that was the meaning of my dream.

Looking worried, he left me alone and went in to talk with his wife, also a doctor. After my treatment, as they often did when I visited them, they served a lovely lunch. When the meal was over, the doctor turned serious.

"You know, Patti, there is something we have decided to tell you; however, it musn't leave this room. We feel that since you seem to have such a strong, deep inner bond with Paul, you are involved, whether you know it or not. We think it is best that you be told what has happened."

Something inside me was feeling sick. I did not want to hear whatever this was, but I also knew I had no choice. The doctor went on.

"When Paul was in Spain, someone poisoned him. He is in very bad condition."

I was stunned. "But . . . but, why? How? Where is he?"

"Gail brought him straight home. He insisted on it. He wouldn't go to a hospital there. I don't know how he made it. He put himself in a trance for the flight home. I've been treating him almost every day. He refuses to go to the hospital even now."

Tears welled up in my eyes. Paulji. Paulji. Oh please, God, no! I choked out the words, "Is he going to die?"

The doctor shook his head solemnly. "I don't know," he said.

"Can you tell me what happened?" I asked softly.

"All we know is that a young man in Spain asked for a consultation, and he slipped something into Paul's juice."

"But why? *Why?*" I asked.

The old doctor looked at me, shaking his head with sadness.

"He heard voices in his head that told him he had to destroy the man."

Apparently what had been mixed into the juice was a caustic solution of some kind. Paulji's stomach had been all but burned out. His heart, severely stressed, was also acting up.

Gail later told me that as soon as they arrived back in San Diego, she took him to a doctor who insisted he go into the hospital immediately. Paulji refused, and the doctor said, "If you don't go into the hospital, you won't live out the week." Months afterward, Paulji would tell this story to me with a grin of satisfaction spread across his face. He said he had pointed at Gail and told the doctor, "That's my nurse, and she's all I need."

I sat quietly, looking at the two doctors for a long time, thinking about it all. The white spots. The syringe. My life force. I must have been used for some kind of a transfusion. I remembered my strange behavior, the trip to San Diego. Now I blurted that story out to them.

They looked at each other and nodded, knowingly. "Even though no one told you, even though you were sure he was in Europe, Paulji was in San Diego, hovering between life and death. You had to be told. At least now you will understand when some of these inexplicable things come up, and you won't think you're going crazy."

I was grateful for their thoughtfulness, but, I was beside myself with grief and worry. I never was very good with timing, but what inner sense of it I did have said Paulji must not die now. He couldn't. There was too much left to do.

I made the long drive home consumed with shock and sadness. How could anyone want to hurt this gentle, humble Soul? Again I thought about the syringe and the transfusion. I did not recall being asked if I would donate some of my life force, but I knew I had agreed.

Oh, I thought, fighting off a new onslaught of tears, I wish it could have been me instead of him. The world will miss him so, but it wouldn't miss me.

That day, once and for all, my puppyhood was finished.

Eight

It was a pale, emaciated Paul Twitchell who arrived in Las Vegas on October 21, 1970, for the Fourth World Wide Seminar. No one, except perhaps his wife, Gail, will ever know the price he paid in terms of pain, energy, and well-being in order to be there with the ECK chelas. I found it difficult to believe he was even going to try and was very upset when I learned of his plans to go, although his decision was not firmly made until a few days before the event.

His life had hung in the balance for nearly three weeks and only then did he begin to rally. He never revealed the exact measures he took to heal himself, but from many sources, including Paulji himself it is known that he had frequent treatments from a doctor and he also used some kind of a trance method on himself. After the critical phase of his illness, he was finally able to take nourishment in the form of protein milk shakes.

The introduction of these milk shakes was a big breakthrough, because prior to them, he had been unable to hold down any food and thus was using up what little strength he had left.

Except for a few members of the Inner Circle, Paulji's poisoning was not known to the world or to his followers. From August until the World Wide Seminar, no word was spoken of his condition. This was a precautionary measure. If he was to survive, he needed an atmosphere of calm, silence, a free mind, and the maximum amount of peace surrounding him.

This wise decision avoided the emotionalism and hysteria of certain people and the well-intentioned desires of many to do something — anything — to help. He correctly foresaw that if the news of his condition leaked out, he would be hard pressed to protect himself from the barrage of psychic healing forces well-meaning people would set into motion. He also knew that many would be thrown out of balance by the knowledge, and this would be a further drain on him. So he worked on healing himself in secret — at least as much secrecy as he could have with so many connected to him inwardly. When his life had begun to ebb away, it was felt in various ways by many. No one knew consciously what had happened to him, but they knew something was not right.

He arrived at the hotel in Las Vegas in a very weakened condition. Unknown to all but those closest to him, he carried a portable oxygen tank and mask in his suitcase, and he had to use it on more than one occasion.

It had been Paulji's habit to speak three times a day at seminars. He usually spoke around ten in the morning, once in the afternoon, and again in the evening session. He held to this same schedule now.

I approached the seminar with mixed emotions. On the one hand, I was tremendously apprehensive about having to give a talk before hundreds of people, since I was barely recovering from my terrible fatigue. On the other hand, I was worried about Paulji and wanted so much for him to be well that I, like many others, seized upon thin air to convince myself he was healed.

Other than the fact that he was pale and very thin, there was no outer clue as to his true physical condition, and he carried on his lectures, business meetings, consultations, and after hours "gab" sessions as usual.

Saturday afternoon I was to be on the program at 2:00 p.m., right after Paulji spoke. The title of my talk that afternoon was: "Put a Little Spring in Your Life." I sat in the wings as he began to speak. I had a tension headache and somebody kindly massaged my neck and shoulders as we listened to Paulji, but half my mind was on my upcoming talk.

All of a sudden there was an unusual quiet in the room. What is he saying? Oh, no!

He was telling the audience of being poisoned in Spain and of his near death and struggle to survive. You could have heard a pin drop. People were crying. The air was so heavy with the shock and emotions of five-hundred-plus people that you could have cut it with a knife.

I already knew the story but was in shock too. I sat there thinking about the jokes I'd rehearsed, my funny, little "up talk." How can I go out there and be funny after he dropped a bomb like that?

It has happened to me so often since then that I am no longer frightened, but rather welcome what I call "the mindless state." Actually, when I am mindless I am far better, or, at least, not as bad as I would be if my mind were all that was being listened to.

As Paulji slowly walked off the stage, the shocked audience applauded him. It was an expression of love and appreciation for the fact that he'd made it, and encouragement for him to keep getting better. Then they introduced me and my delightful, fluffy, little subject, "Put a Little Spring in Your Life."

Completely mindless, I walked out on the stage and looked at the vast circle of unhappy faces surrounding me. The audience could see my smile as I took the microphone, but they couldn't see the muscles violently trembling as I tried to hold the smile in place. Thank God, I had prepared something and had rehearsed it endlessly, because now the talk just spewed out without my having to consider it. I said to myself, the whole thing is going to be a horrible failure anyway, so just get it over

110

with and get off as fast as you can. I started with an opening joke:

> When I was asked to come and give a talk here in Las Vegas, I was very excited. I couldn't wait to tell the family what their mother was going to do. The first one I found to tell was my nine-year-old, Petey. "Guess what, Petey?" I said, "I have been asked to give a talk in a big hotel in Las Vegas." "Gee, Mom," he said, "that's great!" "Would you like to come to the seminar and hear my talk?" I asked. He was quiet and thoughtful for a moment, then he said, "I guess not, Mom. Heck, we don't even listen when you talk at home."

Suddenly, there was an explosion of laughter such as I have never heard at an ECK seminar before or since. One thousand eyes fastened upon me and five hundred hearts drank in the light and funny anecdotes I put before them, including my favorite one about the incurable little optimist who was locked in a roomful of horse manure for a week. When the people who were trying to cure him opened the door, they found him digging away, happily smiling and saying, "There must be a pony in here somewhere!" I told them that this was what I always say when I'm in the middle of a tough learning experience and nothing is going right. That story also brought a thunderous burst of laughter.

Finally, it was over and I left the stage. After-wards, people swarmed around me, hugging and thanking me, many with tears in their eyes. They said they were so grateful that I had been in that spot to lift them out of the sorrow and shock. They poured out so much love and gratitude that I was awestruck.

Later that night I lay awake for a long time reliving the afternoon. When I first realized what Paulji was doing out there, I was very upset with him. How could he do that to me, before my very first talk ever? How could he do that to anyone and expect them to come on funny? He was doing seven or eight talks at that seminar. He had to have purposely selected that time to throw out his big bomb.

A stillness crept over me, then a magnificent realization.

He trusted me that much.

A rare photo of Paulji and author, Chicago,
1971.

Paul and Gail.

With Gail Twitchell after hours at a seminar.

Artist's re-creation of cartoon Paulji sent with the message, "You need more self-confidence."

Paul Twitchell seals which were placed in thousands of books in the Seattle Public Library.

Paul Twitchell

Paulji's valentine from Seattle newspaper days.

It was customary for Paulji to sit on the edge of the stage following his talk and shake hands with all who wished to meet him.

When Paulji and Gail walked through the hotel lobby they were often stopped for handshakes or to autograph books.

One of the pictures Gail took in their Del Mar, California back‐yard.

Paulji, Little Bear, and Big Bear giving the ECK blessing, Baraka Bashad.

Patti:

I said other day the word was "Shraddha" for 6th Initiates — but its really "Shradda" — The Next printing of A Brochure initiation shall be Corrected —

Congratulations — you've made it into the ~~Shraddah~~ Shraddha Circle + Now been saved — Not by the bell, but by the Flip of the Angel's wing —

The letter Paulji wrote after author's Sixth Initiation.

Paulji usually had difficulty attaching his microphone before a talk, causing him to once mutter to the audience, "I'm a philosopher, not an engineer."

Nine

Paulji's room at the Stardust Hotel in Las Vegas was on the second floor of the same complex that my room was in. In order to get to my room from the main auditorium, I had to walk down a street which ran right below his corner window. Then I had to turn the corner and walk about a half a block to the room I shared with another lady.

It was late, perhaps nine or ten o'clock. As I approached the alley behind Paulji's room, I saw a man crouched close to the building across the alley. He was squatting in the dark and staring up at the lighted windows of Paulji's room. I slowed my pace so I could casually pass and study him. Perhaps he was only daydreaming and staring off into space. As I slowly passed by, I studied him carefully. He was smoking a cigarette and was definitely staring up at Paul Twitchell's room.

In retrospect, I can find other explanations for

113

his odd behavior. Perhaps he was a hotel employee sneaking out for a smoke. He could have been drawn to look up at that particular window by something he didn't even understand, like maybe the ECK. I will never know. All I knew was that someone had already tried to hurt Paulji once, and others might possibly wish to harm him too. I rushed to my room, dialed the operator and asked for Helen Baird's room; I would ask her what to do. Helen, who like most ECKists, stays up half the night at seminars, was not in her room. I quickly dialed the room of another Higher Initiate, who was not in either. Not knowing what else to do, I asked the operator for Paul Twitchell's room and Paulji answered.

"Paulji," I said, "I don't want to alarm you. It's probably nothing, but as I passed below your window, I saw a man crouched in the alley. Perhaps someone could take a look."

"Thank you, Patti," he said, "I'll have it checked out right away."

I hung up and sat down heavily, hoping it was all okay and that I'd been mistaken. Before long there was a knock on my door. I opened it to a hotel security officer, who questioned me at length on exactly what I had seen. Apparently by the time the person Paulji had sent got out there, the suspicious person had gone.

About this time one of Paulji's oldest chelas, a woman of about fifty, stormed into the room, screaming.

"How *dare* you call Paul and tell him someone is watching his room!"

"Well," I stammered, "I didn't know what else to do."

"I'll tell you what you did, you just about killed him, that's what! He's up there under oxygen and half-dead."

The woman ravaged me with anger, repeatedly saying that Paulji might die because of me, that there hadn't been anyone in the alley, and that probably I had only wanted to get Paulji's attention. At the very best, she felt that all I had seen was the shadow of a bush or something.

She went on raging, demanding to know why I hadn't called this or that person, people I had never heard of. I could see I had done a terrible, terrible thing, but it wasn't helping anything for this woman to be screaming at me. I apologized over and over. Finally, both she and the security officer left, and I sat there, utterly alone.

I really don't remember much of what went through me as I sat alone contemplating the possibility that Paulji could actually die because of something I had done. There is, however, a limit to how much pain and remorse the human mechanism can stand. I decided that if he did die because of something I did, I would die too; not by my own hand, but from a broken heart.

I sat there for some time, wringing my hands, pleading with all the powers that be to spare Paulji, and smarting from the woman's attack, which I regarded as being semihysterical due to her own fear for him. She was too upset to realize that my mistake was innocent, and that I would die a thousand deaths before allowing one hair on his head to be harmed.

The phone jangled; I seized it. It was the office manager from the ECKANKAR office.

"Patti," he said, "I'm in Paul's room, and he would like you to come up right now, if you can."

I think I was at Paulji's front door before the fellow had hung up the phone. I knocked lightly, and the office manager opened the door to let me in.

Paulji, in blue pajamas, sat in a chair, looking a bit sallow, but okay.

"Hello, Patti," he said, "we were going over plans for the book distribution and some other things. I thought you might like to sit in."

My heart was near breaking.

"Paulji, are you all right? I understand my call upset you. I feel I did the wrong thing, but I didn't know what else to do. I'm so terribly sorry."

He smiled weakly.

"Aw, it's all right. I'm okay."

"Is there anything I can do for you?" I asked.

"I don't think so," he said.

He was rubbing his neck muscles, and I asked if they were sore.

"I've just got a muscle spasm, that's all," he replied.

"Would you like me to massage it a little?" I asked, praying he'd let me do something — anything — to somehow make up for the trouble I'd caused.

116

"That would be nice," he smiled.

Two or three men were in the room chatting with Paulji, while I stood behind him gently massaging the tight muscles. He murmured a few times that it felt good. I didn't pay the slightest attention to the conversation, since all my concentration was on those shoulders and trying to relieve the tension a bit.

There was a lull in the conversation and Paulji addressed me. "I understand that you got told off royally about that call to me."

"Yes," I said, "she was terribly upset, but I can understand that. Boy, she really let me have it."

"Well, don't pay any attention to it," he said, and then chuckled, "Some people get so excited they talk first and think later."

"She told me you were almost dead," I said.

He laughed. "Well, I'd say that was a bit of an exaggeration. Just forget about it, Patti."

I don't remember much more. He asked about my family. He said he had heard a lot of good comments about my talk in the seminar program. Then he appeared tired and we began to leave. Flowers that people had sent to him were all over the room. As I walked out the door, he reached into a big floral arrangement, pulled out a long-stemmed rose, and handed it to me with a smile. I floated back to my room, clutching this treasure. I realized that all that had taken place there was for me. In the midst of everything, he had taken the time to understand that I was nearly destroyed by the events of that evening, and he had made this

117

incredible effort to help me by allowing me to do something for him.

From most accounts by those attending the seminar, it seemed that even though Paulji was pale and drawn at the beginning of it, he seemed to improve as the days went on. There was a general feeling that he was buoyed up by the warmth and love of the chelas assembled to see and hear him. This appears to have been a case of mass wishful thinking: so many people wanted a thing to be so, that it began to appear it was. Even though I knew better, I also got caught up in the wishful thinking, mainly because I so desperately wanted it to be true too.

The following account, which I had probably written, appeared in the November *ECK Monthly Letter* of that year.

> Friday afternoon Paul told a stunned audience of ECKists about his narrow escape from physical death in Madrid this past summer when someone handed him a juice drink which contained some caustic chemical. Three times he nearly left his body for good, and only by putting himself in a deep trance was he able to remain connected to it. It was a long time before he was able to take any solid food and he lost a great deal of weight, some of which he has now gained back.
>
> Paul filled the lecture hall for every lecture and as the seminar wore on he was surrounded by such an aura of love and devotion that one could actually observe him improving in health and spirits by the hour.

This, I believe, is one more example of Paul Twitchell giving people exactly what they wanted. It was his chelas' desire that he be well and happy. Indeed, he did seem tireless. He even sat on the edge of the stage one evening following his lecture and invited everybody in the auditorium to shake his hand. Hundreds and hundreds did. The line wove like a snake around the large room, and some stood in line the better part of an hour for the privilege of shaking his hand and speaking a few words with him. If he was exhausted, he did not show it or speak of it, and he did not leave until the last person had received his attention.

The chelas of ECKANKAR left Las Vegas that year shaken but heartened. Surely no ordinary man with a serious physical condition could have withstood the pressures, hours, and strains that Paulji had endured at the seminar. Everyone returned to their various states and countries reassured and grateful that the terrible experience had come and gone, although they had not known of the danger until it was over.

Ten

Journal entry, November 1970:

When Paulji called, asking me to come down to his office, he said he had not been feeling well. He sounded tired on the phone. My senses told me his condition was not good, but when I arrived, I saw that it was grave.

Before Helen and I got there, I had given myself a good talking to, determined not to put on my nurse's cap; in other words, not to engage in any medical observations. I conditioned myself to forget whatever I knew about medicine. All these good intentions lasted until the moment I saw him. He was so gravely ill that even the most untrained eye would have seen it immediately.

Although I tried not to, I could not help but register the signs and symptoms of his condition. His skin had a sallow, deathly pallor. His wonderful eyes, always so electrifying and sharp, were dull and lifeless. There was a cloudy, rheumy look about them.

His feet and ankles were swollen to almost double normal size. He wore a pair of old, felt bedroom slippers, which he said were the only things that would fit on his feet. He was terribly weak and could barely walk; when he did, it was a slow shuffle that made him seem very, very old. My heart sank, for there was every evidence that the situation was extreme, that Paulji was a dying man.

He had been in his office on the street end of the apartment complex when Helen and I arrived. My face is always a road map of my thoughts, and during the whole visit I fought hard to keep my grief from showing. Paulji's vitality seemed at such an incredible ebb, I could feel none of the power and energy that usually surrounded him. I felt sure he lacked the strength to pick up my thoughts.

My husband, a gourmet chef, had been curing venison for mincemeat pies. The pies turned out spicy and wonderful. I knew Paulji could never eat anything like that, but I brought one for Gail, telling Paulji in a kidding, mock-stern voice, "Now, you stay out of that pie! It'll kill you for sure!"

After we had finished our work, he decided to take Helen and me up to his and Gail's living quarters. He wanted to show us the apartment, which I had never seen, and something they had there, which I believe was a piece of art.

To get from the office to the apartment it was necessary to descend the stairs on the street end; walk through a lovely courtyard of palms and bird-of-paradise plants; and, at the ocean end, to ascend another flight of stairs to the living quarters.

Paulji walked with that slow, shuffling pace. I walked beside him, my left arm linked through his, partially supporting him. As we got to the landing leading up to his living quarters, I began to worry about how Paulji was going to get up those stairs. I was about to ask Helen to take his other arm so we could really support him, when he turned very abruptly saying, "I don't need any help. I would appreciate it, though, if you two ladies would just leave me for a few minutes, because I have to do this my own way and slowly."

Helen and I understood perfectly. We walked to the edge of the sidewalk where we could look out at the sea, keeping our eyes averted from him, a difficult thing. Could he make it? What if he fell? What if he collapsed from strain and died while we stood by, forcing ourselves not to look?

I was torn. Part of me wanted more than anything else to insist on helping him, even if it meant half-carrying him. But the other part knew that he needed something else and, whatever it was, we were not to interfere. And so, our human love, which wanted to take care of him, bowed before a greater love. We had to be warriors, willing for anything to happen as he made his way up those stairs. It was another nightmare. I was certainly having my share of them these days.

I don't know how long Helen and I stood with our backs turned, forcing ourselves not to look, but it seemed about fifteen minutes. Often, since that day, I've wondered, did he go up one step at a time, resting on each one? Or did he sit and scoot himself up backwards on his rump? We'll never know, but he did finally make it. When he called to us, he was on the top landing, entering the apartment. He left the door open for us and he had disappeared into another room. Later, I saw a big tank of oxygen in there and assumed he had used it to revive himself.

He showed us around the apartment, which had a large bay window overlooking the sea. The beach was not the typical, lovely California beach, but resembled beaches I have seen in southern England and up at the Arctic Ocean. It was bleak; there was no sand, only little pebbles which hurt the feet. The pebbles stretched from the water up to large boulders, breakwaters between the sea and the buildings. Paulji's apartment hovered like an eagle's nest above these boulders and the forbidding beach, which was far more pleasant to look at from this lofty height than it was to walk along or bathe in.

One time, Helen and I had arrived early for an appointment with Paulji, and he was out somewhere on an errand. To pass the time, we decided to walk down to the beach and dip our feet in the ocean. In order to get to the water's edge, one had to climb over huge grey granite boulders, a difficult thing hardly worth the effort. The whole landscape seemed to discourage visitors to the sea-side.

Paulji now sat on the living room sofa and chatted politely with us. Terribly unnerved by the cloudy, faded look in his eyes, I couldn't keep myself from thinking about it. Fearing that every minute we stayed put more of a strain on him, we left as quickly as possible.

Because of the tumultuous events and experiences of the past months, I had calmed down and was less prone to spontaneous hugging and overt expressions of affection, but this time, as we said good-bye, I gently embraced him and kissed him on the cheek. Some weeks later I made another entry in my journal:

> I kissed him good-bye that day with a heavy heart, aching with the feeling that I would never see him alive again.
>
> This ominous feeling stayed with me for a week and a half, and then suddenly, out of the blue, it was gone. The cloud of oppression that I had been under lifted, and I had the distinct feeling that Paulji was going to stay with us.
>
> A few days ago he called me, saying he had work for me and that he was feeling much better. He summoned me to his office. Helen said that he was a little miffed that I had brought a pie which only Gail could eat. Helen suggested I bake a pie that Paulji could eat too. I discussed it with Gail, and it was decided that a pumpkin pie with mild seasonings would probably be OK for his digestion.

Bearing his pumpkin pie in hand, I arrived at Paulji's. I must confess, I was ready to believe in a miracle just because I so desperately wanted one, but what hope was there of that? I have had more experience with terminal illness than with blind faith and while my mouth said, "If he wishes to heal that body, he will heal it," my medical mind disagreed: "That body has had it, face facts."

At best I felt that if he were to recover, it would be a long, slow process. But I was totally unprepared for Paulji's remarkable appearance and probably will never recover from the wonder of it.

Every single outer symptom had completely disappeared. This was a Paulji I had not seen before. Not only was he vital and energetic, but his eyes, which had always been magnetic and piercing, now had a clarity, a depth and intensity, that I had never seen before. Frankly, I could not stand to look into them for more than a few seconds.

The afternoon I was referring to in the above journal entry was the afternoon Paulji took me out to lunch after we had completed our work. He was wearing his regular shoes, which I found reassuring. I could not get over his energy and clarity of mind. I felt as if I had just awakened from a terrible dream. As we ate lunch, he looked at me appraisingly and said, "What else have you done besides be a nurse?" This was Paulji, back in form. I had never mentioned to him that I had been a nurse.

Several doctors had also witnessed Paulji's recovery. One of them later said that no ordinary man could have lived through the ordeal that he had survived. No medical knowledge was available that could have reversed the physical conditions he experienced, particularly without hospitalization. Yet Paulji effected a reversal of those conditions right before their eyes. One of the doctors told Gail, "This whole occurence is medically baffling. Regardless of one's training or beliefs, it is impossible to deny that he has powers beyond those of the average man."

The question has been raised, if Paulji had such special powers, why did he not detect that the juice drink in Spain was poisoned? There is no need to go into this in depth here, as that will be covered in his biography that I am assembling next, and will detail all he had to say about the experience. Basically, though, I will say that he had a foreknowledge of the poisoning, but that he would not avoid it for special reasons.

Suddenly the tempo of everything picked up. Another Los Angeles seminar was planned for January 1971. Paulji put Helen and me in charge of planning and running it.

My telephone was beginning to ring more often. Many times Paulji would be on the other end with comments on projects or new assignments. Sometimes it seemed he merely wanted to chat — to touch base. He had a cadre of people now, helping him in the various areas. He gave a great deal of attention to those close to him, showering them with letters, phone calls, and meetings, much as one would water plants. He understood that this personal contact energized them and later confessed to me that he was doing some special spiritual housecleaning with each of us, even in the most casual exchanges. He was also planning to convene a council of future leaders he was grooming, a meeting which would be in March in Las Vegas. He asked Helen and me to plan an agenda for that too.

Paulji had a love-hate relationship with the telephone. It was absolutely essential to his work, but he disliked it intensely. However, he was far more tolerant of it when he was the one dialing. When people called him, he would often answer it with a curt "Yes?" For that reason, even though he had given me his unlisted number, I only called him two or three times in the period of nearly a year. I had a real dread of calling him, of perhaps interrupting him during writing. But I soon discovered there was no need to worry about that, for there were better ways to work with him.

One afternoon, as I sat at my typewriter working on an article for one of the publications, I found, to my chagrin, that I was missing a piece of critical information. Time was of the essence and I had to get in touch with Paulji, but I could not dial that number. He called often, and I found myself considering whether or not I had time to wait until he did. I sat there worrying over it, wishing he would call and spare me the anguish of calling him. Suddenly, the phone rang; it was Paulji.

"Did you want me for something?" he asked quietly.

When incidents like this occurred, I tended to ignore them, pretending that nothing out of the ordinary had happened. I have thought about that event off and on and wondered if he really had answered my thought, or was it just a coincidence?

The next time I needed to talk to him, I tried it out, consciously. I began to concentrate on him, sending him the inner message that I needed him to call me. Sure enough, in about five to ten minutes the phone would ring, with him on the line. This was wonderful. I had solved the dilemma of not wanting to call him up in the very best way. Of course, now I see that I was calling him up anyway — by the inner phone — but somehow that distinction didn't occur to me then. Maybe it was just as well. This was a marvelous way to communicate. For a while it worked every time. But then came the time when I called and called, but he didn't return the call. Finally, I gave up and went on with my project without him. Several hours later, he finally called.

"You know, Patti," he said, "sometimes when you call, my line is busy."

That explained it. I later learned that a doctor had been with him right then and had been giving him a treatment.

Another time, I was rushing out of my house to go to his place for a meeting, when I suddenly realized that I needed to know if he wanted me to bring along some copy for the next issue of the *Mystic World*. There wasn't time for the regular inner call, so I dialed his number. As soon as I finished dialing the last digit and before his phone had even rung once, I heard him say, "Yes, what is it, Patti?"

I began to stutter and stammer. "Well, Paulji," I said, "I dialed, but you answered before the phone even rang."

"Yeah," he laughed, "this phone does that sometimes."

In the first part of 1971, Paulji had set about to cure me of yet another of my mindsets. The color of this piece of glass is: *It is imperative that I always be on time or early*. Some of this he worked out on the telephone.

A strange string of coincidences began to occur. It seemed that every time I had an appointment somewhere, Paulji would call just before I was about to leave the house. It happened before a parent-teacher conference, a dentist appointment, several beauty parlor appointments, and several luncheon dates. I would be ready to go, have my keys in hand, and he would call about something. The business taken care of, he would begin to chat about this or that. I simply could not tell him I had to be somewhere else, because my priorities were straight enough to know that nothing in the universe was more important than a call from Paul Twitchell.

Nevertheless, I would be listening and talking and watching the clock, knowing that my on-time line had just been crossed, and I could not possibly make it to the appointment on time. But I never cut him off. One particularly difficult occasion was when my husband and I were about to leave for some engagement. My husband was more of an on-time person than I and not the most patient man in the world.

We were about to walk out the door when the phone rang. Oh no, I thought with dread. Sure enough, it was Paulji, and he had some business to go over with me. After that was out of the way, he began talking about the Civil War and the generals' strategies. Paulji had a passion for the American Civil War and loved talking about it. He also loved going to the movies. Afterwards, he would do a special ECK-viewpoint review of them. He was current on the political situations all over the world and the forces behind them, and he loved to expound on them. He was also a storyteller, par excellence. I was treated to a large segment of his thinking while time ran out on this or that appointment. It was now happening again.

I could see my husband out in the courtyard frowning, rattling his keys, and getting more and more impatient by the minute. Finally he went out the gate and got in his car. By this time Paulji was going on about a television skit he'd seen on the "Carol Burnett Show," which was about the only show he liked. I thought for sure my husband would just drive off without me, but still I would not tell Paulji of our previous plans. After what seemed an eternity, he said he had to go. I hung up and ran out the front door to face an infuriated spouse.

Breaking up a mindset is not comfortable, but neither is having one. Looking back for the purposes of this memoir, I have seen a common thread running through those lessons that I hadn't consciously noticed as I was experiencing them. A mindset creates discomfort and intense feelings over matters that don't require them. Today, I would not hate a pea-soup green car, although I still would not prefer one. And I'm careful now when I order something large from a tiny color sample that I visualize this color on a whole carpet, wall or car, or whatever it is I am picking out.

For me, to be late was the equivalent of a hanging offense. I have no idea where such an idea came from, or how long I'd believed that, since it had no relationship to how important the appointment was. If I was delayed, I'd break all the speed limits to try and make up the lost time.

When Paulji began to break up this mindset of being on time no matter what the cost, he ran me through the intense discomfort of his inopportune calls over and over again. Sometimes it was like a Keystone Kop movie. I'd be listening to him, looking at the clock, squirming, calculating how to still make the appointment on time; and then, at some point, whether I should call, cancel, make an excuse, or what. I would hold the phone, pace the kitchen, and worry. Eventually, I had been late so many times that I saw what he was doing it for: I was late. So? It wasn't the end of the world. No one ever seemed to be as upset about it as I was. However, until Paulji began making me late, I didn't realize this, because I honestly don't remember ever having been late for anything. It's fair to say I was a fanatic.

Paulji also weakened this mindset through the publications; I was always on a deadline. In those days, the entire monthly mailing to the chelas went out on the same day. Paulji and I had to plan to get our work done and send it to the Las Vegas ECKANKAR office in time for that mailing. Since he was still, at that time, approving everything before it went to the printer, we had to figure on enough time to shuttle the work back and forth between us before it could be printed and shipped to the ECKANKAR office.

Paulji began to use little delaying tactics; I began to nag at him for it. In my own behalf, the office was calling me wanting to know where the publications were. Several times we missed the deadline badly, so the entire chela mailing was late. Since the general manager was not about to give Paulji any flak, I caught hell instead. But Paulji didn't worry about the monthly mailing being late; he was curing me of my panic over being late. At times, his decisions seemed to be clearly arbitrary. Finally, I decided, oh well, if *he's* not going to worry about this deadline, why drive *myself* crazy? I relaxed. If everything fell together in the proper time span, great. If it didn't, too bad. I quit nagging him about deadlines. If he delayed me, I simply shrugged and worked at his tempo. Shortly after I had relaxed and dropped my mindset, he called me with the approval for my final layout and said, "You know, Patti, you really need to work harder to meet your deadlines."

I swallowed my giggles and said, "Yes, sir!" very smartly.

Before leaving the subject of promptness, I need to introduce the paradoxical nature of this whole story. In all the time I knew him, I never knew Paulji to be late for anything. On the contrary, he was usually early. Over the years I have had all kinds of appointments, all over the world, with three different Living ECK Masters. I hardly recall them ever being late; more often than not, they arrived ahead of time.

Paulji's impeccability in everything he did was fascinating to observe. He was meticulous about remembering details. If he said in casual conversation that he'd do a thing, he always did it. If I said I would, he always remembered, although sometimes I forgot. It didn't matter whom he was meeting, if he respected the person enough to make the appointment, he showed that by being there on time. Once I heard a behavior therapist discussing chronic lateness. He said that people who are habitually late often use this as a way to impress upon others their importance. I don't know if that's true, but if so, it seems to be a losing game, since in my experience the most important people I've ever known were habitually on time.

There was another strange phenomenon concerning Paulji and the telephone. My discussion group met in my living room twice a month. As soon as we would begin that week's discussion, the phone would ring. I would excuse myself and Paulji would be on the line. The class always knew it was him. It was an electrifying experience for them to continue the discussion while Paulji himself was connected to the house by telephone. As usual, I would not think of trying to get away from him, so he would talk on and on. We went through Lincoln's presidency and funeral cortege, socialism, Marxism, advertising gimmicks that had hypnotic effects on people, and many other topics. The class ran itself without me, but always with a portion of its attention fixed on the kitchen where I stood talking on the phone. We all decided that no matter what this phenomenon of Paul's untimely calls was all about, nevertheless it was a wonderful thing.

It was in connection with my class that Paulji also provided one of my biggest moments of spiritual growth. I had begun the class as a discussion group. While many other classes were studying the Satsang Discourses, we didn't; we kept right on discussing anything we wanted to. This was due to the fact that Paulji had used the term "discussion group" when he first asked me to start the class. I figured when he wanted us to begin studying the discourses together, he would inform me. I was still pretty literal about everything in those days.

It is a premise of the ECK teachings that the Master is always with each chela. I naively thought that meant that Paulji, the person, knew every single thing I was doing. It was some time before I realized that he could, if he wanted to, but the human being, Paulji, couldn't possibly have had the time or the interest to keep up with every minute thing each one of us was doing.

One day we were talking on the phone and I said something about the discussion group. Paulji exploded.

"Do you mean to tell me," he said, "that you people still have not started a regular Satsang with the discourses?"

"Uh, yes, that's right," I said shakily. "I thought you knew."

"No," he said with irritation, "I did *not* know. I want you to get that class on discourses right away."

I said I would.

Later, as I thought this over, I began to get very upset. How could he not have known? My God, he was calling the house during almost every class!

He didn't know? He didn't even know that? I wondered if I had been misled. My mood grew darker and darker. I became angry and very disillusioned and got the distinct sensation that I had been lied to. The thought that I had been misled by Paulji burned in me like a fire, and the pain was

136

very deep. Suddenly I didn't know if I wanted to have anything to do with this path, after all. I withdrew from everyone and seriously considered quitting.

One day I had lunch with Helen. I told her what had happened and that I was not sure I wanted to stay. She didn't try to fix things, but merely suggested I not do anything rash. Just take a break for a few weeks and give myself a chance to work it out. I knew that because of her closeness to Paulji he would find out what was happening, but I didn't care.

I couldn't lead the next class. How could I talk about this thing called ECKANKAR when I wasn't sure I believed in it anymore? I had a member of the class be a substitute teacher that day, and the class went well, in spite of my crisis. I was careful not to let any of the class members know my true state of mind. I was responsible enough to know it was my problem, not theirs. To my relief, Paulji didn't call in the middle of that class.

A day or so later I walked down to the beach and sat on the sand, looking out at the sea and wondering just what Paulji's game was, anyway. Was it all a lie? Was he a charlatan? Had he conjured this whole thing up? As careful and doubting as I had been, had I still ended up believing something that wasn't even true? Yes, I thought, somehow that seems to have happened. I believe I will have to quit.

Having made this decision, I sat and stared into the breaking waves.

Eleven

Although my present predicament contained some of the elements of a tantrum, it was a serious spiritual crisis. Outwardly, Paulji kept his hands off. I know he felt the pain I was experiencing, and knew what a critical time it was for me. If he was giving assistance on the inner, I was not aware of it. On the outer, he simply withdrew while the crisis played itself out in me.

I have come to believe that saying the right thing at the right time is a spiritual art. It is something that we all remark upon and marvel at. We smile and say, "Isn't being a channel for Spirit wonderful?" Almost from the beginning, the chela finds out about this and works with it, and it truly is a joy. But to me it is almost a minor art. As strange as it sounds, saying the right thing is really not so difficult. The real art—the truest act of golden consciousness—in my book, is knowing when to say nothing. And this is precisely what Paulji did. Knowing he had been told about my dilemma, I wondered if he'd do something outwardly to retrieve me. He didn't; he ignored me completely. He backed off and waited to see what I would do. If this was going to throw me, so be it. Now was as good a time as any for the test, the perfect thing for him to have done. I needed to work it out myself.

I sat looking at the waves crashing on the shore, hugging my misery. It seemed that my whole concept of ECKANKAR had been like that of a beautiful sandcastle. And now, along had come this gigantic wave, and whoosh—my sandcastle was no more. Well, it couldn't have been much, if one wave could demolish it. Still, there was something nagging at me. I had had many realizations and a lot of growth as a result of that fragile sandcastle, hadn't I? I began to backtrack my experiences to see just what it was that had attracted me to ECKANKAR and had kept me with it so long.

For a reason that I no longer remember, I continued to work it out in keeping with the sandcastle analogy. I saw that Paulji had given me all this information, these inner experiences. I had taken what I wanted from them, and I, myself, had used them to fashion this particular castle. Inside this castle, I had, step-by-step, constructed a stairway that led to the top, up and out. *Up and out*. A long stillness reigned in me as that thought settled in.

Up and out. If I fashioned the stairs, then I also must have climbed them . . . up and out. And then what? Well, then the big wave came, and the castle was gone. And what of me? Had I crashed to the former floor of the castle?

I thought and thought. Was I really a crushed, soaking heap in the sandy remnants of my once glorious castle? Was I back to the Patti who went off to the rented cottage by the sea in 1968? No. I was in the spot where the stairs had ended; I was up and out. I am who I am, not who I was when all this began . . . no, not at all. My stairs are gone . . . true . . . but they got me here. With rising excitement, I saw that it didn't matter if I hadn't seen everything exactly as it was; I had seen it as I needed to, in order to get up and out. *In ECKANKAR, everybody makes his own unique sandcastle.*

I thought about my idea to leave ECK, and then I started to laugh. I realized that I could never leave ECK. I am ECK. I might walk away from this organization, but wherever I would go, I would take It with me, because It is not something I have, or think, or believe, or understand. I am It.

I sat there for a long, long time — grinning, laughing, seeing exactly what Paulji was waiting for me to see. With this new vision, I was freer than I had ever hoped to be. And I was overcome with admiration for, and gratitude to, Paul Twitchell, who had made this priceless gift mine. It was awesome, this accomplishment of his.

Everybody makes his own unique sandcastle. No two are ever the same. Likewise, everyone is his own path in ECKANKAR.

I didn't feel the slightest guilt for this episode of backsliding in my unfolding. I knew I had come out of it with a quantum leap in my Soul journey. I knew Paulji was going to be utterly delighted. I sighed, picked myself up off the sand, and headed back—to work. I was very glad that I had kept all my misgivings to myself.

That afternoon, I pulled out my work to look over what had to be done next. I found a question for Paulji and rang his inner phone. Very soon he called. We picked right up where we had left off, as if the heartbeat had only given the slightest pause in its regular rhythm. To my knowledge, we never once mentioned my crisis, but carried on as if it had never happened.

The January seminar in Los Angeles was a big success. There were some who went to great expense to be there because of a rumor that it would be Paulji's last. They came, so to speak, to pay their last respects. He, however, was quite robust, although he did not venture out on his own in the hotel as much as at past seminars. I believe he also cut down the number of lectures he did. But, other than that, it was business as usual.

Several of the members of my Satsang class had young boys about the same age as my youngest son, Peter. The boys had discovered a wet bar in the back of the seminar room and immediately went into business. When the break came, they sold glasses of water to the thirsty attendees. I believe they were charging a nickel a glass. By the time Sunday had rolled around, they had made about $2.30. Since they were so young, no one pestered them with the problem that the water they sold wasn't theirs to sell. I asked what they were going to do with the money; they said it would be a surprise.

It turned out that they had somehow learned the number of Paulji's room, had knocked on his door, and, when he opened it, they gave him the $2.30 to help run ECKANKAR. Paulji treated them with deep respect; he couldn't have been more touched and grateful. He responded to the gift as if a delegation had arrived with half a million dollars. While he never had children of his own, he was always extremely thoughtful around them. Many of his lectures dealt with the teaching of children and of the adventures and misadventures of his own childhood.

It was at this January seminar in Los Angeles that he told about a time at school when he had gotten in trouble with his teacher. A disciplinary note had been sent home to his parents, who scolded him severely and ordered him to take a bouquet of flowers to the teacher to make amends. On the way to school, classmates teased him for carrying a bouquet. He launched into a fight, and the bouquet was completely devastated. He said that by the time he got to school there were only two limp flowers and some broken stems, which he dutifully presented to the teacher.

Paulji grinned with satisfaction when he told this tale. The ruined bouquet didn't bother little Paul, for he had no regard for this particular teacher anyway.

Many of the stories he told at that seminar were for children, and there were a lot of children there. The majority of the stories concerned his being naughty, showing that even the Master was once a kid who got into mischief. The children loved the stories and repeated them often.

I have one other memory of that Los Angeles Seminar which still makes me laugh to this day. There once was a woman (I shall call her Mrs. X) who studied under Paulji in the very early days, who has long since left ECKANKAR. This woman seemed to be omnipresent in those times. I don't know a really kind way to describe her: she was demanding, manipulative, and pushy. She always managed to maneuver herself into an audience with Paulji and was forever trying to get things out of him for her own advantage, without working for them. It seemed impossible for him to escape her, and she practically drove him crazy.

One evening, Helen and I took Paulji away from the hotel to a restaurant for dinner. When we returned to the hotel parking lot and had emerged from Helen's car, Paulji spotted Mrs. X and her husband getting out of their car, which was parked between us and the door into the hotel. Although Paulji had spotted her immediately, she had not seen us.

"Wait!" said Paulji sharply. Not knowing what he was talking about, we both froze and looked around to see. Paulji ducked down behind the back of Helen's car. He whispered loudly, "I don't want to run into that woman!" Once we saw Mrs. X, both of us quickly joined Paulji in a crouch behind the car. Helen and I were working over-time to squelch our laughter. Mrs. X and her husband entered the building, while Paulji waited until he was sure they had disappeared into the bowels of the building before he'd enter.

"I simply cannot stand that woman!" he said. And then he grinned and added a quiet after-thought: "I love her though."

One afternoon, we were having lunch together and Paulji gave me a new insight into what he was doing with his books. A new book was coming out—a novel. I said I was excited about the pros-pect of reading his latest work. He raised one of his eyebrows at me, a mannerism he had before delivering some surprise.

"You are not going to like this book, Patti," he said.

I shot him a questioning look. I couldn't con-ceive of Paulji writing a book I wouldn't like. He went on to explain.

"You have to understand what it is I'm doing," he said carefully. "Every book I write is not meant to appeal to every individual. Some people like novels, some like histories, some are interested in health or science, others get more out of poetry or music. No matter what I write, I am introducing the same truths, but I do it in different ways for different interests. This one is just not your cup of tea."

Sure enough, when I read the book, I did not care for it. This gave me a valuable insight, and it fit in closely with my vision of the sandcastle. I did not need to be enthusiastic about every single facet of Paulji's work, because some of it simply didn't apply to me or my own particular path within the path. Each one of these revelations brought me closer to the Patti I had met in my beauty spa dream. I was becoming more and more who I really am, and my powers of discrimination were increasing daily.

I have seen some chelas struggle with this faculty of discrimination, while others seem to have no trouble with it at all. For myself, I saw that ECKANKAR is valid. It works. What Paulji promised would happen, did happen. But because I found my own truth in it, and used it as he meant it to be used, does not mean that everything he said applies directly to me. Nor is it a requirement that I embrace everything I see and hear, just because it came from Paulji. This is the overview, the discrimination and detachment that he wanted each of us to achieve. I do however embrace the fact that ECKANKAR enfolds an incredible potpourri of truth, and that it has something in it for every type of person. I'm not obliged to accept all that's in it, unless it is for me. There are people who run into difficulty with this because they bring along patterns from former religions or disciplines. They demand that others must subscribe to every tiny detail of a belief as they do or be lacking in faith. Never mind that a lot of what we end up subscribing to in those situations is useless to us, or worse, places chains around our ability to question and learn and experience.

Also involved in this issue is the fact that our experiences and learning times are unique to each of us. We are not all doing the same thing at the same time in the same way — or in the same sequence. I know of people who took up ECKANKAR because they read *The Tiger's Fang*. I was not able to handle reading that book until I had studied almost two years. I still have little interest in *The ECK-Vidya*, the book of prophecy and cycles, while many, including my husband, are fascinated by it and work with it. Prophecy is just not my cup of tea — at least not right now. Maybe some day I will find myself deeply involved and learning it a mile a minute, but right now it holds little interest for me and that's perfectly all right.

Paulji got into the habit of talking to me about his life, giving me information for the new biography he wanted written. I always tried to tape these conversations. By his own admission, he was not an easy child to raise. His home circumstances seem to have been both supportive and abrasive for the person he would one day become.

147

Paulji's family lived in Paducah, Kentucky, which is at the confluence of three rivers. When he was a child, the city was a major artery for the transportation of goods by water. Paulji's father, whom he loved deeply, worked for a shipping firm, but was also knowledgeable in metaphysics and Eastern thought. His stepmother, with whom he had a totally miserable relationship, was part American Indian as well as a devout Christian. There were two other siblings: Katie, who always sided with little Paul, and Howard, who always sided with his mother.

When Brad Steiger, with Paulji's help, wrote *In My Soul I am Free,* these names and places were changed. Paulji said that he did not want people bothering what family he had left. Once his father and his beloved sister had passed away, however, he didn't seem to have any ties left in Paducah. It was inevitable that his origins would one day be discovered, and since others already have, I now feel no restriction about using the information he gave me.

There has been some controversy about Paulji's birth and true familial relationships. One story is that he was the illegitimate product of a dalliance between his father and a local woman, that his father maneuvered the circumstances so that Paul could be raised within the family, and that his stepmother, Effie, hated him because he was a constant reminder of her husband's affair.

Another story has it that he was indeed the biological son of Effie, and that the animosity she felt for him had more to do with the fact that he followed Eastern religious practices, along with his father and sister. He was, by his own admission, a very bright child and an independent handful.

If he was Effie's biological son, this had to be the only thing the two had in common. His alienation from her was every bit as complete as if he had truly been foisted upon her to raise. I don't really know which story is true, nor do I see it as an issue. One thing I do know, however: Whether he would fashion a parable as a teaching example, or use a memory from his actual life, Paulji was constantly recounting "stories." Whether he was relaxed, off-guard, or reminiscing on any subject, I never, ever, heard him refer to Effie Twitchell as anything other than "my stepmother." He was often totally caught up in the humor or the point of his tale. He would be laughing and his words racing along. Surely he would have slipped at least once if he'd really seen her as anything other than his stepmother. If she actually was his biological mother, the rejection of that fact was complete and total in his own mind.

Although I cannot conclusively verify one or the other of those stories, it is a fact that he wanted a new and more accurate biography with a lot more detail in it, and that he wanted me to write it. For his part, he would allow me to interview him and would furnish any information of importance for the project. To give an idea of how he worked with me on this, I will include an entry in my journal made at the time of these sessions.

In the course of many conferences, dinners, and lunches, Paulji has, in a casual manner, talked to me of his childhood, naval service, training in India, as well as his newspaper work, and what life is like on a day-to-day basis for a twentieth century Adept in the United States of America.

As the work progresses, delicate pictures emerge of Paulji, of the relationships that were most significant in his life. I am also treated constantly to the deep, warm love and bantering camaraderie between himself and his lovely Gail. All in all, I am seeing him as few people have the privilege to . . . yet, he remains unfathomable. In a manner of speaking, I know Paulji . . . I can communicate with him in a friendly, relaxed manner . . . but I do not understand what he is all about even yet. He will not fit into any classification that I am familiar with.

He is frank and open and unbelievably generous with replies to whatever questions I ask. Whenever I ask him something, he answers it directly and without hesitation. Sometimes he crinkles his forehead and thinks hard, trying to remember a place or time, then sparks forth with his remembrance of it. Many times he will excuse himself and run into another rocm. When he returns, he has a clipping, a photograph, or some other documentation for the story he is telling me.

I am sometimes struck by how common, how ordinary this man and this experience is. Sometimes I think I am on the verge of clearing up the whole enigma, so ordinary has everything become between us. Then, like a puzzle nearly

150

completed but suddenly reshuffled, the whole thing will rearrange itself. Everything that contributed to this understandable picture appears to be either meaningless or so steeped with meaning and significance that it cannot be a real-life story, but a parable.

He told me many stories about his childhood and most of them contained some reference to the powerful alliance that existed between himself and his sister Katie. She was his friend, ally, fellow conspirator, healer, teacher, and champion. She is the one who taught him at a very early age to Soul Travel, to consciously get out of his body and look back at it.

The stories that he told, especially to the kids, at the Los Angeles seminar in January 1971, were of the Paul and Katie Show: Paul ditching school, Katie writing excuses for him, and generally looking after his welfare. Paulji did tell me once that it was Katie's purpose in this lifetime to look after him, to see that he survived. In addition, she was often his spiritual tutor during his younger years.

Following the January seminar, Paulji and I settled into the pattern which would last until his translation (the term used in ECKANKAR for death). I was editing and writing for the two publications. In addition, I was working on gathering data for his new biography. Whenever we had a meeting, whether it was lunch, in his office, or at a seminar, I had my tape recorder monitoring him. Several times when I did not have it, he would begin to tell stories that were autobiographical.

151

We decided that since one never knew when these things would come tumbling out, it was better to leave the recorder running nonstop. In the beginning the tape recorder seemed to make him a bit self-conscious and somewhat ill at ease, but gradually he became accustomed to it and recognized its usefulness. Before he translated, he himself was making sure someone had the recorder going, even when I was not around.

In addition to letting me tape material on his life and experiences, he also undertook training me to be a writer. This meant teaching me to get an overview on whatever I was investigating. Some of the things he taught me furnish an insight into how he himself must have worked.

From time to time, he would send instructions to me in a letter. One of my most interesting assignments came in the form of a book. It arrived in the mail with the following instructions:

> Patti:
>   I want you to read this book and as you do it, project your consciousness into the mind of the author as he sat writing it. When you are able to do this, you will find things in your reading that completely escape the ordinary reader. It is not at all a difficult thing to do.
>   PT

This was the format of most of the correspondence I received from him. It was always hand-written in black felt-tip pen, which I believe he used because he wrote so many letters every day, and it took little energy and pressure to write with it. He always put "Patti" at the beginning, very rarely the formal "Dear Patti," and it was always signed "PT."

Although the task of projecting into the author's mind as he wrote sounded difficult, I lost no time in trying it. The book, whose title and author I can no longer recall, was a pseudo-scientific treatise or study on some aspect of parapsychology. The author kept referring to it as a research documentary, but I soon found myself in his head and found it was no such thing. This fellow was an angry man with an axe to grind, whatever the subject, which he meant to deal a dirty blow. Because I could see this, I was more objective. I could see that he had subtly treated certain material as *a priori* truths which were not that at all, and he cavalierly referred to certain other ideas as superstition, with the inference that his opinion of them was a proven fact that everybody knew and agreed upon. He was, in truth, so clever about it, so subtle, that, in the past, I might have bought into it. Now I could see that this man was no more an objective researcher than the Pope is an objective theologian. I was amazed at what I had learned and returned the book to Paulji with a note:

Paulji:
    I tried your technique on this book. It really works. I saw that this man was incredibly angry about something and he was bent on destruction. Thanks for the

lesson. Next time I have to go into a
writer's mind, I hope it is not such a
garbage can.

Patti

Paulji loved it!

Twelve

Sometime early in 1971, Gail Twitchell called to relay a message from Paulji. Gail has (as did Paulji) an exceptional sense of humor, dry and light. A conversation with her was always fun and full of easy laughter.

"Well," she said, "I guess we're moving."

"Really?" I responded, rather astonished. I hadn't had a hint of it before this.

There was something funny about this. I could tell, because Gail is one of the few people I know whose voice can smile. When she is unwinding a funny one on you, the smile in her voice is unmistakable. Her voice ripples musically, and you have the sense that at any moment, she'll just have to burst into laughter.

"Paul is packing," she said, beginning to giggle, "so I'm sure we will."

She said he didn't have a new place yet, nor did he even know when they were going, but he knew

155

they would be moving, so he was packing. Gail thought this hilarious.

I don't know how long it was after he finished packing that he found and rented the perfect house in Del Mar, California, but soon they were settled in their new home and I was visiting them.

Gail and I had a lot of fun together. I loved her sense of humor and the gentle way she'd badger Paulji. She kept him grounded, and he literally adored her. Often, when I came to their home, Gail and I would visit and swap cuttings from plants in our yards, while Paulji worked. I recall several blackberry and fern plantings she gave me that nearly took over the gardens at my house. The blackberry bushes even invaded our neighbors' gardens.

Gail and her twin sister grew up in rural Washington State. Paulji often said that there wasn't anything Gail couldn't do. She had driven a huge tractor as a child and was pretty fearless. She is petite, and over the years I teased her about how strong she was for such a little thing. I began to call her "Mighty Mouse," which refers to a cartoon character mouse fashioned after Superman.

Gail was in college and working in the Seattle Library when Paul Twitchell came to her attention. Every week, he would check out and return innumerable books. Inside them he placed little mini-review bookmarks: either a "Paul Twitchell Sour Grapes Award" or a "Paul Twitchell Seal of Approval." At that time, Paulji was a reporter and columnist for the *Seattle Post-Intelligencer* and a staunch nonconformist. I think he was naturally that way, but during his years in Seattle, he worked hard at a public persona that reflected and enhanced this characteristic. He was already practicing the art of public relations and self-promotion that he would soon need for something far more important. In the meantime, Seattle was treated to a funny and fearless Paulji. One of his eccentricities in that period was colorful sports caps. He told me he had over a hundred of them and wore a different one to work every day. I don't know where they all went. By the time I knew him, he had only a Greek fisherman's cap.

In his spare time in Seattle, Paulji was writing and developing what would later become ECKANKAR. He fascinated the young coed working in the library. Before long they were seeing one another socially. Gail was very interested in the spiritual subjects Paulji discussed, but she had no background other than Christianity. He agreed to teach her. He began writing letters to her on various topics that he felt would be beneficial to her understanding. He wrote her two-paged, single-spaced typed letters anywhere from once to four times a week. Gail often didn't understand what he'd said in a letter, but he would not allow her to ask any questions until the end of the week. Then they would meet for tea, and she was allowed to ask all the questions she wanted.

"Some of that stuff was so far beyond me," she once confided with a laugh, "that I didn't even know how to frame a question to ask."

These letters were preserved, and two volumes of them have been published for the general reading audience. The third volume is filled with such potent material that it is studied in monthly discourse form by advanced students in ECKANKAR.

Their friendship blossomed into romance. About that time Paulji moved to San Francisco. Later he came back for Gail, and they were married.

It was in San Francisco that Paul learned he was to bring his work out into the public. So he withdrew from his newspaper career and began to write full-time. Gail made this possible; she quit college and went to work to support him while he formed the outer body of his work and systematized the teachings. He promised Gail that once he was established and earning money again, she would be able to finish her education.

When I first met Gail in 1970, she was a psychology major at San Diego State College. Paulji was by then traveling a lot, going off to this or that seminar. Because of her studies Gail often had to stay at home, but whenever Paulji made his overseas journeys, she always accompanied him. She was invaluable in keeping track of tickets, reservations, bags, etc. He tended to be a bit absentminded about some of the physical realities.

For instance, I remember the day we had worked all morning. At home, he always worked in his stocking feet; shoes seemed to annoy him. As lunchtime approached, he said, "Well, let's go eat, I'm hungry." I packed the tape recorder and put my papers in my briefcase. Paulji got his keys and pulled on his suit coat. He held the front door open for us, then closed and locked it. Partway down the porch stairs, I turned to look back at him and collapsed in giggles. He looked inquiringly at me.

"Uh, Paulji?" I said, "Do you think it might be a good idea to put on shoes before we go?"

He looked down at his stockinged feet in complete amazement, laughed, and went back into the house for his shoes.

Paulji called me to say that they were moving. I chuckled and asked, "Have you found a place?"

"Yes," he said, "and you're going to love it!"

He was right. The house they had rented in Del Mar was on the side of a hill. The living room looked out at the sea through beautiful pine trees. In back were patios and terraces with all kinds of ferns and flowers and space for Gail to grow vegetables. The house was one story. There was an office for Paulji right in the house, so he didn't have to leave home; it was much more convenient for him.

When I arrived Gail gave me the grand tour, while Paulji periodically called to her to be sure and show Patti this or that. Other than a houseboat he had lived on in Seattle, I think Paulji loved this place more than any other place he had lived. Even though it was on a residential street, the way it was made and the large amount of land it sat on gave it the sense of isolation he loved. Rising above the pines, it had the effect of an eagle's nest, high up in the trees.

My painting of the master and chela walking on the lighted path through the dark forest hung on the wall over the dining room table. This was Paulji's favorite spot to sit and talk; it was also where we always worked. On this occasion he invited me to take a chair and offered me a cold drink. It was a ritual that I was given a glass of fruit juice or mineral water. I remarked to him that I felt very honored to have my painting hanging there. He looked around, searching the shelves along the wall for something. He said, "Pat Henderson did a sculpture of me — a bust — and I want to show it to you."

He called to Gail, "Where is that bust of me that Pat Henderson did? Bring it here, will you? I want to show it to Patti."

Gail soon arrived with the bust; Paulji frowned at her in mock-seriousness. Suddenly he was playing in a way I had never seen before. He began a proclamation.

"Let it be known, here and now, that at no time, I repeat, at no time, is this bust of Paul to be anywhere but on display in this dining room."

Gail and I were laughing so hard we both had tears in our eyes. This was a game I would see played again and again — Paulji dropping into the role of a great and important man, poking fun at pompous postures. The game was always punctuated by my giggles because it was so ludicrous.

160

Paulji, I was learning, was the most powerful spiritual man on the planet at that moment. He was also the shyest, most gentle, and almost child-like being I have ever met.

One day, shortly before I arrived, a small bird had crashed into the glass window. It had fallen to the ground, unconscious. Gail told this story:

"Paul was working inside when he heard the bang. He went out on the front porch and discovered the bird—I believe it was a bluebird—knocked out cold. Paul was yelling at me, saying, 'Come quick, hurry!'

"I couldn't figure out what was wrong. I really thought something terrible had happened. Although I was on the telephone, I hung up in the middle of a sentence and went tearing outside only to find him so very concerned about this bird.

"'You've got to do something,' he said. I got an eyedropper and some honey water and went out to revive the bird, not knowing really if it had even translated yet or not.

"We gave it some honey water and pretty soon it began to shiver and shake. Then it opened one eye. About that time Paul became the great public relations expert and said, 'Get your camera quick!' So I went charging back to get my camera while he was waiting by the bird.

"I aimed the camera. Just as I pressed the button, the bird flew off. Paul stood there and shook his finger and said, 'You call that gratitude?'"

Another time there was a mouse in the house. Gail, tired of the messes it was making, set a trap for it. One morning, there it was, caught in the trap by one of its legs. Paulji released its leg and carried the mouse out to the garden. As he was doing this he gave it an ECK lecture. He said that the mouse looked at him as if to say, "You must be completely out of your mind!" When he let it go, Paulji said he felt the mouse was more happy to escape that lecture than it was to escape the mousetrap.

Paul and Gail had no children but lived with several stuffed teddy bears and Gail's German Shepherd, Theodore von Dog, also called Teddy. All were major personalities. The atmosphere around the Twitchell house was very light and gentle — the description I search for is akin to "highly refined." Everything was done in subtle ways. It was here that I really saw the child-selves of both Paulji and Gail; and my own child-self began to learn to be. This required one to drop the solid, heavy world and enter a world where anything could be so.

The Twitchell teddy bears (at first there were two) were called Big Bear, or just plain Bear, and Little Bear. These bears had distinct personalities; I soon got to know what to expect of each of them. Big Bear was the main bear and he was sort of the boss. But Little Bear was feisty and was never at a loss for a new trick to get on top of things. One day I found Little Bear in a baseball cap, holding a stick. Gail told me he had had to get his own "Rod of Power," because he'd been having trouble with people bossing him around.

Often the bears acted out issues between the Twitchells that might have been more difficult to resolve if left to the humans alone. This included me a few times. Once I had written a long report to Paulji and arrived to find Big Bear bent over it, wearing Paulji's glasses. I was told that since it was so long, Bear was going to condense it for his friend, Paul. Just then, Bear crashed over on the table, and Paulji shrugged. "I guess it was too much for him." After this, I kept my reports short.

Once, while on a trip, I saw a tiny stuffed bear; it was really puny. It did not have a lush coat or anything to make it attractive. I immediately felt sorry for it. Silently I said, I don't think anyone will buy you, but I know a family that likes bears. Perhaps they would adopt you.

I sent the little fellow to Paulji and Gail with a note saying that this was an orphan, whose name I believed was Nearly. At least that seemed right because he was *nearly* a bear.

Nearly was taken in and found among the other bears from time to time, although Gail said Little Bear was very miffed at first. The bears would sometimes be propped up in front of the television so they could watch their favorite show, which I feel quite sure was "The Carol Burnett Show." There was also a family newsletter, edited by Big Bear that came out in the household periodically. In other homes the wife might write notes to the husband about chores that need doing and things to remember. In the Twitchell home, these were usually the feature items of the family newsletter.

In her "Points About Paul," a tape Gail recorded for me, she said this about the newsletter:

"I helped Big Bear put out *The Bear Facts,* our home newsletter. After the first issue, Paul sat down with Big Bear and pointed out all the errors he had made in setting up margins and the complete setup of the news. . . . He told Bear that if he was going to do it, he was going to have to do it right. And he really meant it. It was no joke. If it was going to be a family newsletter, Big Bear was going to have to be just as precise and professional as anyone else.

"And, of course, Big Bear agreed."

When I listened to Gail's tape I found myself thinking about that day, so long ago, when I contemplated my mutilated newsletter dummy in that cold room. Would it have gone easier for me if I had known that Big Bear would receive just as much discipline on the home front for a very small circulation publication?

Paulji told me of a time he had to drive to Las Vegas on business. Gail was staying home due to her class schedule, but was concerned about his driving such a long distance all by himself. To mollify her, he said he would not go alone, he would take Bear with him. And so he left in his blue Volkswagen, Bear sitting on the front seat beside him. Paulji told the story with a great twinkle: "Everything was okay until I got to the border where they inspect your car for any fruit or vegetables that you might be carrying across the state line. That inspector must have really wondered

164

when he saw this rather distinguished-looking, older gentleman with a teddy bear sitting next to him." I have no doubt Bear was also wearing sunglasses as he always wore the right costume for every occasion.

I was always pushing Paulji for more photos of himself for the publications and he would always groan. He had a dislike of being photographed which was never explained. Once he agreed that I could come down with a loaded camera, and he would hold still for some shots. I had a brand new, self-advancing camera which took wonderful pictures. I put in a roll of thirty-six color exposures.

When I arrived at his house, I cajoled Paulji into going out in the beautiful backyard. Grumbling and mumbling he finally wandered out. I pointed the camera and said, "Smile." He frowned. I took the picture anyway. As soon as an exposure was made, the camera was supposed to automatically advance the film to the next frame. Suddenly, there was a great whirring. My camera was advancing non-stop. It got quiet. I looked. It was now on exposure number seventeen. I took another shot of Paulji. Whirrrrr. We went to number twenty-one.

"Paulji!" I yelled. "Stop that!"

He grinned. I shot again. Whirrrrr. I was now at number thirty. I got two more shots of him and the game was over. I was a little annoyed. I said to him, "I know you hate to have your picture taken, but don't you think that's a little rude?"

He looked wounded and innocent. "I haven't done anything," he protested. Of course when I got home and put in a new roll of film, the camera worked properly. Meanwhile, Paulji must have felt a little sorry for poor Patti who was, after all, only trying to do her job. He had Gail get her camera, and he posed for more pictures. He told me by phone that he had made more pictures and was mailing them to me. He also said there was a special one in there for my private collection. When they arrived, I anxiously opened the package and fanned through them, looking for the special one. There it was: Big Bear and Little Bear were sitting facing the camera. Big Bear wore a badge that said, "I love ECK," and Little Bear was wearing one that said, "I love Paulji." Behind them, peeking over their shoulders, was Paulji. All three were giving the Master's open-palmed blessing, which means "Baraka Bashad," or "May the blessings be."

At the time of this writing, American society is infatuated with the teddy bear. There are bears and bear-decorated products everywhere one looks. Back in 1971, teddy bears were only something children slept with; something you read about in *Winnie the Pooh*. I sometimes wonder if Paulji had anything to do with the current bear rage. If he didn't, he was certainly ahead of his time.

Thirteen

In the previous chapter I have given some stories and insights about the Paulji and Gail Twitchell that I knew. About a year after his translation, in an effort to preserve a record and capture how very human Paulji was, I asked Gail if she would tape-record some of her memories of him and of their life together. What she had to say beautifully captures the essence of his personality, and of the special love between them; the recording gives a poignant, lovely picture of Gail herself. She began by talking about Paulji and his love for all living things.

"I remember one time we were sitting at the breakfast table. Looking out back, we saw a sick or wounded butterfly. We immediately gave the butterfly a name so it would have an identity. Paul picked up the little butterfly and put it on a green leaf. We proceeded to check 'Madeline,' I think it was called, every few hours—all through the day and all through the night—to make sure that she was where no birds, dogs, or cats could get near her. Madeline was soon able to take off on her own, thank goodness.

"I think probably our favorite animals were the dogs: Teddy (Theodore von Dog) and Parsley. Paul was very fond of Teddy, but it was really a challenge since Teddy was always my dog, no matter what. Paul would put Teddy in his car and take him down to the store and buy him an ice cream cone, but he would still come home Gail's dog. In the beginning, no matter what Paul did, he could never win Teddy's love.

"Sometimes we would let Teddy loose and he would wander off. I would be sure that Teddy had run away. I would be so upset that Paul would go out in the car and drive around and around and around. Usually he'd find Teddy. Teddy, of course, probably thought that Paul was lost and that he'd found *him* and brought him home.

"Later, Teddy had a genuine feeling for Paul. I don't know if it was because of all of the attention Paul gave him or because Paul really liked him. Of course, Paul did let him in the house.

"I always said that Teddy was an outside dog, but I would come home from school and there would be Paul, sitting in the middle of the bed, watching the evening news on TV, surrounded by the bears. And there, right in the middle of all of them, would be Teddy, which was quite a horror to me. And so, they would all get bawled out royally.

Paul would look kind of cross-eyed at the whole family and say, "Mrs. Twitchell knows best." And that would take care of it till the next night.

"Parsley was a big, fuzzy grey-and-black over-grown poodle who lived somewhere in the neighborhood. He had so much hair you could never be quite sure whether he was coming or going.

"The way he got his name, Parsley, is a funny story. One morning when Paul and I were having breakfast, I looked out back and saw this funny-looking dog. I was chattering away and Paul was reading the paper. I was talking about . . . oh . . . my garden, and my carrots, and the parsley, and the dog out back. Pretty soon I said, 'Paul, you haven't heard a word I said!' He looked up and said, 'Oh yes, dear, you were talking about a dog named Parsley.' So the name Parsley stuck.

"Parsley was probably happier to see us come home than he was to see his own master come home. In fact, Parsley would always come over whenever he heard our car drive up. He would just *happen* to be waiting on the front or back porch. He would never bark, never. Oh, he was so shy. Finally, we told him that he'd have to be more aggressive if he was going to get along in this big world. And so he would finally bark for Paul, but it took all of his energy and all of his courage.

"Paul and I used to feed Parsley. Then we put little ECK stickers on his dog collar and sent him home. We always wondered if his owner was puzzling over what kind of little journeys he was taking."

* * *

"Paul loved fresh flowers, just as I did. He made it an unwritten rule or law that he would see that there were always fresh flowers in the house, so it would be nice and cheerful. Once I went out and bought him some flowers which he appreciated. But later he said, 'Don't I do a good enough job?' I realized then how very sensitive he was and that I had hurt his feelings by going out and buying the flowers myself, because it was his own special task and he enjoyed doing it. This was part of his way of 'taking care of Gail.' "

* * *

"Paul and I always wrote each other a note if either one of us would be out of the house when the other returned. If Paul was asleep or busy when I went out, I always wrote him a note and he did the same. They were always silly little notes, like telling him to have a happy day.

"I remember one note when I wanted to buy a piece of marble for a candy board. I went to a mortuary. I told him I had gone out to buy a tombstone. Paul almost framed the note, he thought it was so funny. He said he thought that was very economical. If anything ever happened, he could just have it engraved and save all that money. I know some people would think it terrible to even say such things, but Paul thought it was terrifically funny.

170

"After he had translated, I found all these little notes I had written to him; I thought he would have just tossed them away. But I've come across envelopes full of them, boxes full of them. He used them as bookmarks. Apparently, he never parted with one of them because they're all right here. I think it shows how very sensitive and romantic he was."

* * *

"Paul always picked out clothes for me or some kind of little gift. He never went to a seminar or on any little trip that he didn't bring me something that he had picked out himself. He loved to do it. And he had much better taste in clothes than I did. He could tell if the color was right or the size was right just by looking at it in the window.

"He always had time—even if he just went to the grocery store—to buy something special that he thought would make me particularly happy. So, of course, I always rushed out to help him unpack any groceries or carry in any sack. I would exclaim over every item—it was a really joyous sharing. I totally, thoroughly, and sincerely enjoyed it. No matter how busy he was, he still had time for me. Even if, when we went to a movie, he sat and wrote notes all through the movie, at least he took the time to go with me."

* * *

"Paul was very sensitive. He was very sensitive about what people said. He was very vulnerable to anything that was negative. If you had a negative thought, or thought something would not work out, you certainly never approached Paul saying, "Well, that's a bad idea," or "I don't think it will work." You just didn't do that. At least after you got to know him, you didn't do it. If you could approach him saying it was the greatest idea ever, that you knew it would work, that it was fantastic—then it would come true. But if you put any negative thoughts on it, of course, you broke down the whole idea. He was extremely sensitive to this. He would become very upset if he heard other people doing this. They could correct him and they could suggest better things, as long as they didn't break it down or put negative ideas to it."

*　　*　　*

"Some people think that Paul was a very cold man, but he wasn't. He was the most sensitive man I've ever been around. He wasn't a man who always had his head in the clouds. His favorite type of music or show was musical comedy. We both enjoyed musical comedy. We both felt that if we went out, we wanted to be entertained. We liked 'The Boyfriend' and saw it on the stage four or five times. Even though it was a silly little musical, we thought it was very entertaining. It was a way to get away from business.

"Paul always said that the first requirement for hiring anyone was a sense of humor; that if the employees didn't have a sense of humor, especially in dealing with the spiritual work, it was just impossible. No matter how intelligent, how spiritual, how great they were, unless they had a good sense of humor, they would never survive. I don't think very many people were really aware of Paul's *extremely* dry sense of humor. We would go some place, Paul would say something, and I would be the only one in the room laughing, while all the people were looking weirdly at me. What he was saying was just so fantastically funny — yet no one else got the joke."

* * *

"I think Paul had an incredible way of reading and putting ideas together. Most people can read books and explain or report on them. But Paul could read many different books and put it all together. For example, he'd read books on Russia, then some on economics, religion, etc. Then he would go back and correlate the economic situation, the historical setting, the political setting, and the religious setting. He could say how they all fit together and what caused what, and why the situations were what they were. I think that his ability to do this is probably the most important aspect of his genius.

"Paul was very quiet and very patient — to a point. If he wanted something he would say, 'When you have time, would you do this?' Which meant, I'd like to have it done immediately. But until someone working with him realized this, it was very difficult. I remember one secretary who thought that when he said, 'When you have time to do this' he really meant when you have time. He would say, 'Is it ready yet?' and she would say,

'No.' Pretty soon he said, 'Well, you're fired.' The whole thing was very calm, very efficient, but she was no longer there — it was his way of working."

*   *   *

"Developing me into an individual was something Paul really delighted in. I don't think very many people really realize this. He said he was fortunate that I didn't have a lot of bad ideas so he didn't have to untrain me. I was really open, so he could teach me all these new things. But he did want me to be independent. It has only been in the last year, since he's been gone, that I've had a chance to put all that he taught me to work, because while he was here, there was an unwritten rule that there would only be one speaker from our house. I told him that I would never do anything that would lead people to say, 'Well, Paul Twitchell can't speak; maybe Gail Twitchell will.' I said, 'As long as you're here, it's up to you to have complete control without me entering the picture. All the power and authority must come from you.' So, as I said, it's only been in the last year that I have been able to put into effect the things he taught me about standing on my own two feet."

*   *   *

"I was always excited when Paul came home, even from the grocery store. There was never a time when I was home that I didn't go running out to meet him and let him know how glad I was to see him. And he appreciated it. It was a great

174

sharing between us. We had nicknames for each other. Only at the seminars did he call me Gail. I called him Paul only in the presence of others. Other than that, if he called me Gail, I thought, Oh dear, now what did I do?

"Paul was very quiet but in his own way he let people know when he was upset. As for the telephone, he's been known to hang up on more than one charming telephone operator. He always said he'd rather have more service and less charm. You could see the twinkle in his eyes when he really enjoyed something, and you could tell just by being with him — without any words — whether he was upset or not. He was very exacting. Once he said something, it would be that way. That was it. There was no argument.

"When we'd go to a show, he would drive his car and I would drive mine, in case he decided he wanted to leave in the middle of the show, or if I decided to go shopping or something afterwards, he would be able to go home. He used to think it was funny because we would drive up in our separate cars, park in our separate spaces, and go running to hold hands. You could just see people thinking, 'She must be sneaking out of the house to go to a movie with him.' And, of course, Paul thoroughly enjoyed that."

*　　*　　*

"Years ago we used to practice ESP, different kinds of mind control, different kinds of psychic games, just so he could show me how they worked. And he was an excellent teacher. If I wanted something from a grocery store, I never had to write out a list and give it to him, I just had to think of what I wanted and he would bring it home. The only thing that he didn't ever get right was the type of ice cream I wanted. I always said it was because he brought home the kind *he* wanted.

"He trained me so well I never had to look in the mailbox to know what was there. I always knew ahead of time. I always knew ahead of time what was going to happen. I could look into the future as far as when he was going to translate, when I'm going to translate, and what's going to happen. When my brother was translating . . . I would not advise him not to have an operation, even though I knew he was going to translate when he did have it. I could really stand back and watch these situations without interfering."

*   *   *

"Paul went through a stage of never sending out Christmas cards—that was several years ago, not recently. He went through a stage where he wouldn't shake hands with anyone—he had this current flowing so heavily. I remember the first time I shook hands with him when I met him in Seattle. I thought I'd been electrocuted. I didn't think it was a bit funny. I didn't understand what it was all about, and I thought, this guy's really weird—maybe not so weird, but certainly different. I shook hands with him for six months— that's shocking in more ways than one. Of course, toward the end, with all that current draining out so heavily in his work, I don't think that shock was there.

"He went through stages when he didn't want his picture taken at all, to stages when he would tolerate it. Of course, it always would show when he didn't particularly want it taken.

"He went through some very difficult times and some very happy times. But he still remained a very private person.

"As I said before, Paul was very patient with people — to a point. They were allowed to do something wrong and they were allowed to make a mistake — once. But they had better shape up, because once he told them it was wrong, if they didn't change, that was it."

* * *

"He was very concerned about the people who went to the early seminars, especially the young kids. I remember when one young man went to a seminar in Chicago and didn't have enough money to get home. Paul insisted on buying him a bus ticket. When some chelas were trying to work their way through college and having a bad time of it, he anonymously helped quite a few of them. He had a great feeling for education. I remember when a friend's secretary wanted to go to college. Paul offered to pay her — give her enough work so that she could finance her whole education. Any money spent on books or education was perfectly okay as far as Paul was concerned. He set no limit on spending such money."

* * *

"Paul had a great admiration for good music and good art. He liked original paintings. He liked to be surrounded by artistic beauty and good music. He liked to play his phonograph when he was running from one of his three typewriters to another. He liked to watch television at the same time. He also liked to lie in bed and read a book with a box of crackers propped up on his tummy. Afterwards he'd wonder where all the crackers went. He couldn't imagine that he could get so engrossed in a book that he would finish off the whole box and not even know it.

"One time — I think it was in Cleveland — he bought me a couple of chocolate frogs. They're called Freddy Frogs, and they're still sitting in the refrigerator. I used to have a chocolate lamb Paul bought for me around Easter one year. I got up one day and the lamb was gone. It had almost become a pet to me, and I asked Paul what had happened. Well, he kind of fidgeted a little, and then he said he didn't know. I looked at him strangely. He said, 'Well, I got so hungry, and there was nothing in the house to eat, and I just had to have something, so I ate a . . . a lamb, a whole lamb, last night.' I looked at him kind of cross-eyed and said, 'Well, ya' know, if the Freddy Frogs go, you're gonna be next.' So, I'm happy to say, the frogs are still here."

* * *

"There was an incident in Seattle where Paul really taught me to stand on my own two feet. We were going out one evening, and I said to Paul,

178

'Shall I wear my coat?' He said, 'No, there's no reason to wear your coat.' So I didn't, but when I got home I was absolutely numb. I was so cold I was almost frozen, and I was a little bit, really disgusted. I said, 'Now Paul, you knew it was going to be cold out there. Why didn't you tell me to wear my coat?' He just looked at me kind of blankly and said, 'Well, it was a decision that you could have made yourself.' So I decided then and there that whenever I can make a decision for myself, I won't ask anyone else. And that's what Paul expected people to do. At the same time, he wanted to be informed of what was going on. He didn't like people just going out and doing things in his name and not telling him."

* * *

"Paul was a pretty good cook; pretty good in the sense that if he really wanted some cornbread and knew he shouldn't have it, he would wait until I went to bed. Then he would sneak out to the kitchen and make a batch of cornbread. I remember he would also boil eggs if he wanted some hard- or soft-boiled eggs. He would put the eggs in boiling water and go back to the typewriter, thinking that he'd be through when the eggs were done. Several times the water would boil out of the pan, and the eggs would absolutely explode, just like little bombs. We'd have eggs all over the ceiling. Can you imagine hard-boiled eggs up in the beams in the ceiling, several times! And can you imagine Paul up there trying to clean them off so I wouldn't know what happened. That was even funnier.

179

"Paul was usually quite finicky about what he ate. I would ask him, 'What do you want to eat?' and he would tell me, and I would gladly go fix it. Sometimes by the time I would get it to the table, he would decide he was no longer in the mood for it, and he would just dump it down the drain. At first, this would really distress me. I would think, Oh, what can I do? But after a while it didn't make any difference. I'd just find something else to fix for him. But I could never make him a cup of tea. No matter what I did with the tea, it was too strong or not strong enough, or not the way he liked it. I don't care whether I used loose tea or tea bags or what. I don't think I ever made him a cup of tea he was really happy with."

* * *

"He had a very fine sense of taste and smell. We could always tell by the fragrance when any of the saints, especially St. Theresa, were around. He could easily pick up the fragrances of different individuals, so we could usually tell when she or St. Francis, or someone else, was around."

* * *

"Once I went car shopping for Paul. I think it was when we bought his little Volkswagen. I went in by myself and the salesman said, 'Well, I can't talk to you, you will have to bring in your husband. We'll talk business with him.' He wouldn't say anything more to me. I told Paul that he'd just have to go in with me, although he really knew a lot less about cars than I did. So he went with me

180

and sat down. The salesman started talking business and Paul said, 'Oh, I don't know, you'll have to ask my wife about that. She takes care of all the business.' This didn't particularly make the salesman overjoyed. But Paul delighted in it."

* * *

"I think the only real disagreement Paul and I ever had was over our bank account. And that was because I insisted that it balance right to the penny every month when I checked it. Paul would write checks if he had to, but he could never remember what amount he wrote them for. He would just write on the check stub whatever he thought the amount might have been, if he had some memory of it. Sometimes he wouldn't even write figures in at all. Then, when it would come time to balance the checkbook, it'd be just absolutely impossible to figure out.

"I finally went to the man in charge at the bank and asked him what I could do. Paul kept saying, 'If you really want to, you can figure it out.' But I was absolutely desperate, so I went to the operations manager at the bank. We worked and worked and worked and still couldn't figure it out. So the operations manager and I both decided that we'd just have to close the account and open a new one. Then if I kept track of it myself, it wouldn't be a problem.

" 'Well,' Paul said, 'you know, that's not right. If you really want to do it, you can.'

"So then I went to the bank president and told him the same thing. And he just shook his head and said he couldn't figure it out either. But I think that was the only thing Paul and I disagreed on — trying to straighten out the bank account. We never had an idea of whether we had $1.00 or $1,000. If the check didn't bounce, then we'd figure we still had money in the account."

* * *

"Paul was really very conservative, even though people who didn't know him thought that he had a lot of weird ideas. But politically, he was very conservative. He didn't like to see sloppy people; he liked to see them neat. Before he would come to the dinner table, he would always wash his hands and usually change clothes. This came from his childhood training in the South. He was much more conservative than most people realize.

"He used to wear his hair just a little bit long, but that was because of a birthmark he was sensitive about. He told me if he cut his hair a certain way it covered the mark. Otherwise, his hair would have been much shorter. He thought it was important for the people representing ECKANKAR to look sharp and deal with the public to the very best of their ability, to be the very best representatives they could be. And even though he taught freedom, he knew that you had to be socially acceptable in order to be effective in the world.

"As I mentioned, Paul would have nothing to do with balancing the checkbook, yet he had absolutely no problem dealing with thousands of students and thousands of dollars. It was only the

bothersome little things that he'd rather have someone else take care of. But when it came to figuring
out the business, he had great insights and he had a
reason for everything he did. I'm not quite sure
that in the moment he said or did something, that
he even realized what it was. But he knew that it
had to be done that way and that's the way it was
done. Once he said, that's it — that was it!"

*   *   *

"I was just thinking about the people that Paul
had to deal with. It seems like people in authority
or with authority really annoyed Paul — especially
if he thought they were treating the little people
rudely and abusing their authority. For example,
he knew that if the airline people really wanted to
help, they could. But usually they would just
shove people aside. Paul made sure that they
didn't shove him aside. Of course, he would speak
up about the way they were treating others too.

"I remember he used to get very annoyed with
airline pilots. Every time he'd close his eyes, they
would tell him we were over the Grand Canyon or
Crater Lake or passing somebody's swimming
pool. He used to call the stewardess and say, 'If
he's our tour director, who's flying this plane?' Of
course, the stewardess didn't think it was really as
funny as I thought it was.

"Paul could be very outspoken at times. I
remember when a lady smoking a cigarette came
up to him at a seminar in Chicago. She said,
"Master, may I speak with you just a moment?"
And Paul said, "No, not with that cigarette in your

hand." He walked off. That's how he was. He wouldn't speak to her — no discussion, nothing.

"I remember traveling with Paul through Arizona and the Grand Canyon years ago on one of our very earliest ECK lecture tours. He had a very strong feeling for anything that had a thunderbird on it. He would bring home little vases, key chains, and things with thunderbirds on them. He was always very close to such things. Even his little bank that he kept all of his quarters in had a thunderbird on it."

*   *   *

"People never thought that Paul was nervous about going out on a stage. Yet, I think there was always a certain amount of tension and nervousness before a lecture. This is one of the reasons I usually tried to stay with him until he went to the lecture room. The last hour before a lecture was always the hardest on him. Then, after the lecture, he would be in a very good mood and would want to have people go back to the room with him and talk. That was his real lecture — after the main lecture when he could express his deepest thoughts and get to know his students.

"I remember we took Little Bear with us to Chicago. Paul put Little Bear in a chair and turned on a TV set so he could watch a movie while Paul went down to lecture. When we came back several of the older chelas, all in their sixties, came with us. Of course, Paul had to march over to the chair and ask Little Bear how the movie was, what it was about, and if he had enjoyed it. I wish you could have seen the expressions on those people's faces as they wondered if they were supposed to say something to Little Bear also. Paul thoroughly enjoyed it."

* * *

"Paul took very good care of me. Yet, at the same time, he really let me go out and explore on my own. I remember when we moved into the Del Mar house. The bedroom had no bed lights in it. I told him I really didn't want to spend the money on an electrician, that I would rewire the room myself. I know nothing about electricity. All I know is how to put a plug in the wall and that's it. I told him that if I got a book and learned how to do it, I thought everything would be okay. I said, 'Would you just check every fifteen minutes to see that I'm still surviving and breathing?' He said, 'Sure, no problem.' It didn't really upset him at all. So, I rewired the bedroom and the living room. The living room light blinks kind of funny once in awhile, but other than that it works very well. It didn't upset Paul to think I could be electrocuted. He wasn't going to interfere with my freedom in any way.

* * *

"I think, in some ways, the more Paul knew a person, the less he had to say and the less he did say. When he was getting to know a person, he felt compelled to do a lot of talking. But then the more he knew someone, the quieter he could be. Then he really became himself. I know we had

185

such great communication that talk really wasn't necessary.

"As I have often mentioned, Paul was extremely sensitive. If he thought he hurt my feelings, or I was unhappy, he couldn't tolerate it. And if we had one harsh word I would go off to my room and he'd go off to the office, and always, within five minutes, we were running down the hall to meet each other. He couldn't tolerate thinking that he had hurt me because he said that I always had such a happy spirit; that he had seen so many people with broken spirits that he didn't want that to happen to me. And he said that I always bounced back and was so happy. He appreciated me for being happy from the inside out."

Fourteen

I had traveled a very long distance from the Patti who had stood before Paul Twitchell with her knees knocking together to the woman who could spend an entire day with him, sit in a restaurant with him, order corned beef and cabbage—and then eat it. I did become comfortable with him, but there was always, right at the edge, a sense of awe. I had fallen into a mode which I can only describe as awareness with detachment. That is, I worked, played, dined, and laughed with Pauji—as a friend. Still, there was always the counterpoint melody that this was a man different from any other I had ever known. If I thought about that too much, if I put too much attention on that reality, the other part would cease to be natural and fun.

Some of the things that we were doing were quite extraordinary. Yet for the most part, I had to discipline myself to forget that. The most difficult part of my training was over, that of my high energy and opinions. Now, the teaching was speeded up.

Although I was spending a great deal of time with him now, I never did get over his eyes. Sometimes a sort of dreamy gaze would come into them. I always felt he was looking into eternity. Whenever this would happen, he was in some other mode. He might begin talking to me about civilizations and the teachings of all religions. He would expand into overviews about the history of the planet. There were times when I would think, my God! you can look in his eyes and see creation . . . you can catch a glimpse of a sea so vast, so endless . . . and then the waitress would come and take our order.

Any question or incident could be a trigger for Paulji and send him into this mode. Gail once told me that one night Paulji had gone along with her to do the grocery shopping. In the middle of the supermarket he had switched channels and was explaining in brilliant focus about one of the communist countries and how the political, economic, and religious systems were responsible for what was happening. They walked down the aisles, with Paulji following this very lofty train of thought. Gail was more concerned about doing the shopping and not about what was happening in the communist country. She said, "Paul, Paul, hey dear?" He paused in his reflections, "Yes?" "Uh, what color of toilet tissue shall I buy?" She said Paulji looked at her and it was as if she had heard the most deafening thud. She could practically hear him coming back down from his lofty mode of thought.

"I can't believe you did that!" he said to her, shaking his head. She tried to get him to continue with his discourse, but he could never finish telling her what he was talking about. Gail said it taught her a lesson she never forgot.

Sometimes Paulji puzzled me. It took awhile to figure out what he was up to. Even when I thought I did, I was never absolutely sure. But the time came when I began to feel very much like an extension of him, rather than merely a student.

I would awaken some morning and be thinking that I really should do an article on such and such for one of the publications. I would go to the typewriter and work it through. Sometimes I would be finished or right in the middle of it when he would call and say, "You know, I've been thinking. We ought to say something about so and so." It would, of course, be the piece in my typewriter.

He had asked Helen and me to get up an agenda for the Youth Council, the leadership meeting he wanted to have in Las Vegas in March. Several times Helen and I met and tried to work something out, but the fact was, such an event had never taken place and we had no precedent from which to draw our ideas. A couple of times we asked him what he had in mind for this meeting, if he could give us some clue to help us with our plans. He would be evasive, saying he didn't know yet. Still, we were supposed to be putting something together. It was very frustrating and we couldn't agree on anything.

Finally, the time was getting close. Helen and I got together at my house and decided, come what may, we had to get an agenda. No matter what it was, we would have to go with it and present it to Paulji. Thus decided, we started to bat around all kinds of ideas. Slowly a plan began to emerge, a basic framework within which we could work with the group over a three-day session. By the time we'd called it a day, we had a fairly good outline of how it could go. Later that afternoon, Paulji called me.

"Hello, Patti," he said. "I've been thinking, and I believe I know what I'd like to do at that Las Vegas meeting."

"That's incredible!" I laughed. "Helen and I have been working all afternoon, and we have come up with some ideas."

I was stunned that after all this time, Helen and I had finally come up with something and, at exactly the same time, he had too. I was also a little concerned that we might have differed greatly in what we had created. I asked him about his ideas, so I could compare them to ours and see how close we'd come. Instead, he said, "I'd like to hear what you two have."

I read our proposed agenda. He made a few adjustments and said that it would be fine. I hung up the phone and was thoughtful for a long time. Hunches or impressions were stirring very deeply within me. Which came first, the chicken or the egg? My inner sense said that since we were working with the higher consciousness, and since our work was for Paulji, we must have been in "his part of the house." Either he figured it out and we were then freed, or he wandered into this area of his own consciousness and found a solution being worked out by others for something he wanted. Because of things that happened later, I do believe that there were times when Paulji simply ran my consciousness as another body for himself.

After he had called me, I don't know how many times, to tell me to write this or that piece, only to find I was in the middle of it or already finished, he must have figured we'd passed another milepost. He wrote to say that he did not have to see any of my articles or layouts before publication. I was to handle the whole thing, and he would do his critique of my work after it was printed. This, of course, was the supreme compliment. It was such a degree of trust that I couldn't even be euphoric, so awesome was the responsibility. Nevertheless, I feel it had a lot less to do with how well I was doing the job and a lot more with how closely my vision had merged with his own, how responsive my inner self had become to his creative processes.

This may sound a little spooky, but it really isn't. This kind of affinity and inner bond is possible for anyone who establishes a true relationship with the Inner Master. The main difference is that most people use the inner impulses and insights to effect a positive, spiritual approach to their everyday life and affairs. In my case, they were used to aid Paulji in his physical-world task. When I would begin one of his projects without being told on the outer, the idea would come to me like any other idea. I always thought that I had thought of it myself, until I would hear from him that he wanted it.

But there was an unusual blending of our consciousnesses. When I now look back at old issues of the publications and look at some of the things I am positive I wrote, I would swear I could not have written them. The language, the ideas, the presentation is pure Paulji. Anyone who was familiar with his style would be certain he wrote it. In fact, I am not certain he didn't. There is one article that I feel I must have done, but when I read it, I cannot find anything of me in it.

Even as we were working together on the daily nuts and bolts of ECK, I was already trying to write his biography. The preface in this book explains why this never got off the ground. But I was trying, even while he was still here.

One morning I sat down at my typewriter about nine o'clock and began to write. I was completely lost in my work. Occasionally I would get up and do something else briefly, then I'd go right back to the pages. After I had been there for about two hours, the phone rang. I got up and answered it. It was Paulji.

"Well, hello there, Miss Patti, what's new?" came the soft Southern drawl.

Just as he spoke I looked over at the kitchen clock. It said, 3:30. I was immediately confused and disoriented. I found myself struggling for words. Paulji repeated his question.

"Paulji! The strangest thing has happened. I started working on this new book at 9:00 a.m. I feel as if I've been here no more than two hours, but the clock says it's 3:30! What time do you have?"

"It's 3:30," he said.

"I can't understand that *at all!* I know how much time two hours takes. Paulji, I have lost a whole day. It went by and I didn't feel it or know it or experience it."

He laughed. "Patti," he said, "that's because of the state of consciousness you were in. When I wrote *The Tiger's Fang* the same thing happened. Three days went by and I thought I had been there only a few hours."

"Did you write that whole book in three days?"

"Yes. That's what happens when you are in the other worlds. I know I must have gotten up and taken care of some of the body's needs, but my consciousness never paid attention to that part, so I don't know what my body was doing while I was working on that book."

This kind of thing happened, sometimes only once. It seemed as if the experiences were nothing more than catalysts to draw information out of Paulji; they taught me and gave me material for my books. I never lost a whole day again.

I can hear some of my readers wondering, "What became of the writing Patti did that day?" Nothing became of it. It definitely was not another *Tiger's Fang*.

At this point, I would like to introduce you to one of our typical work sessions. Though dominated by good, hard work, they were always seasoned liberally with wonderful, healing laughter. In February of 1971, Helen and I joined Paulji and Gail in Del Mar.

Paulji, Helen, and I were seated around the dining room table. Gail wandered in and out, but generally was close by and joined in the conversations. Spread out on the table were all kinds of projects that Helen and I had brought to go over with Paulji.

My ubiquitous tape recorder sat in the middle of the table. Parsley came to the sliding glass door and peeked in at us, wagging his tail. He was anticipating a handout from Paulji, who always gave him a biscuit or something to munch on.

It was Paulji's habit to pet Parsley, talk to him a few minutes, give him his treat, and then send him off. (One night when Gail wasn't home, Paulji couldn't find a treat for Parsley. Rather than disappoint him, Paul gave him the only thing he could dig up—a frozen lamb chop.)

Today, perhaps realizing there was a new audience for him, Parsley refused to leave on cue. Although Paulji adored him, when Parsley's time was up, Paulji would no longer acknowledge his presence. Paulji turned his back on the door where Parsley waited and ignored him.

We discussed many things, including my working with the printer directly so that Paulji could be freed of all those calls and visits.

Paulji then reached into a stack of his own papers and handed some to Helen.

"All right, Helen," he said, "here're some goodies for you. In there are several columns that I used to do for the newspapers I worked on in Seattle."

"Did you give her the good ones, like the one on the police department?" Gail asked with a twinkle in her eyes.

"I don't know if I found that one." he said.

"Conveniently," she grinned.

Paulji chuckled and explained. "One time we got stopped by the Seattle police. I don't know what we did. Gail said, 'My God, what do you do to attract these police like flies?'"

"They tailgated you for *months!*" she said to him. Then to us, "It was because of an article he wrote about the police department being a necessary evil. Every time he got into his car, there was a policeman behind him."

Gail looked over in his direction.

"Did you show them the valentine?"

"No," he said, "I thought that was awfully silly."

"It was cute!" she protested.

We asked him if someone had sent him a valentine. He said no, that he had made one up during that same period in Seattle. He continued to dig around in his stack, pulling out samples of his Seal of Approval and Sour Grapes Awards. Gail brightened.

"I remember those," she said. "I remember all the books he used to read. If he didn't like one, he'd put in the Sour Grapes one. He had a stamp made and he stamped these seals on little pieces of paper and slipped them inside every book he read — and he read a lot! I worked at the library desk where Paul returned all those books. The librarian who inspected the books had to go through every page of every book that was returned to the Seattle Library. Those little papers were everywhere!"

Paulji handed us a clipping. "Here's a column I did on pollution," he said. Then he left the room. I read the clipping and burst out laughing.

"That was back when Paul had time to write funny articles — when his incredible sense of humor really came out," Gail said.

We were talking about his articles when Paulji came back to the table carrying something.

"I found those things," he said.

"What were you looking for?" Gail asked.

"Valentines."

He handed me a letter-sized piece of paper. An artist had taken Paul's standard caricature — the face in the checkered sports cap that appeared on the Seal of Approval and the Sour Grapes Award — and had drawn beneath the face a chubby cupid's body. The cupid was holding a file and was sharpening an arrow on it. We all examined the valentine carefully. Then there was an explosion of laughter. Paulji sat stoically, seeming only to endure it, but he was enjoying himself hugely. He absolutely loved a good laugh—even if it was on him.

After we had recovered from the valentine and had settled down, I said, "Paulji, these old columns are *great!*"

"The rebel!" he said succinctly, and then added, "I sure didn't like society."

"Didn't?" Gail raised her brows.

"Don't!" he conceded with a laugh. "But I like you ladies. How about me buying you all some lunch?"

As I wander through my memories of Paulji and my experiences with him, I pick and choose the ones I feel will be of the most interest to the person who never met him, but would like to know about him and what it was like to work with such an individual. The memories come onto the pages in a distillation of time. I think it's important to note that my entire days and nights were not consumed with Paulji. I had a normal family life, a houseful of boisterous teenagers, and one preteenager. I was coping with them, my husband, a German Shepherd, parent-teacher conferences, and a conventional lifestyle. My family life was very important and it gave me balance.

Paulji, while consuming my daytime hours, was very considerate and protective of my family.

He loved all of them and always loved to hear my stories of our various family joys and sorrows. He called me almost every day but never in the evening when he would have interrupted our family life. That was the family's time, and he was meticulous about preserving that for me.

My days began by getting the children off to school and my husband off to work at his automobile agency. As soon as the last person had left, I went to the dining room where my typewriter was usually set up and began the day's writing, editing, layouts, etc. On other days, Helen and I, or I by myself, would have an appointment in Del Mar with Paulji. I would leave about 9:30 in the morning, arriving at his house by 10:30. We would work nonstop until lunchtime. Usually Gail would be there and would join us for lunch. Gail is an excellent cook, and a few times she prepared lunch for us — always a delicious treat. But mostly, we went out to eat, generally to a hotel in La Jolla, which was Paulji's favorite spot.

One day, Paulji and I went to this restaurant alone. There was a light rain falling. As we entered the parking lot, instead of parking the car as I usually did, I pulled up to the entrance, which had an awning, so he could go on in without getting wet.

"I'm going to let you out here, Paulji, and then park the car. I don't want you getting sick. We have to get a lot more miles out of you," I said, laughing.

He laughed too, and got out. I parked the car, ran through the rain and met him inside at the reception desk.

Apparently this act of thoughtfulness and my half-kidding remark had touched him very deeply. Two days later I received a letter in which he mentioned the incident; he said that if everyone could look at it that way, it would save a lot of the wear and tear on him that was caused by people who didn't realize he had physical limitations.

Quite frequently, I would do or say something and it would just pass by at the time, but he would not forget it. A day or two later I would get a letter which indicated that he had obviously examined the incident under a microscope and was now elaborating on its deeper meaning and long-range significance in the whole scheme of things.

After lunch, we'd return to his house, sometimes to work another hour, sometimes to just call it quits and I'd go on home. Every time I would leave, Paulji would walk me to my car, chatting and seeing me off. He always made sure we finished early enough for me to be home to greet my children as they returned from school.

Paulji appreciated the fact that I had a family and another life away from ECK. He worried a great deal about his employees who lived alone and never did anything outside their jobs but activities that dealt with ECKANKAR. He saw a serious danger of them getting out of balance by this introverted behavior. This principle of having interests besides ECKANKAR worked wonderfully for me. My husband was not interested at all in ECKANKAR and wanted nothing to do with it. Because of this, I had a vacation from it every evening and all weekend — with the exception, of course, of the times when Paulji sent me to a seminar or workshop. When this happened, it took some adjustment on the homefront, and there were a few heavy squalls which I have detailed in *Hello Friend*.

Overall, though, considering how much of my time and attention was being consumed, it's almost miraculous that my involvement with the ECK work didn't have more of an impact on my family. Over the years, my husband and I attended hundreds of functions and went on trips with his automobile industry associates, and not one of them ever had the idea that I was anyone in the world but Mrs. Pete Simpson; that suited me fine. It was an interesting phenomenon. Perhaps the subject of my spiritual activities didn't come up because I didn't want it to, or maybe that's the way things are in the circles of important, dynamic businessmen. I do not recall ever having been asked what I did with my time, but had I been, I would have given an evasive answer. I did not want my two worlds to mix. As it happened, when my husband died in 1981, his employees were quite shocked to discover that I knew my way around a corporate boardroom and also how to keep a corporate minute book.

In 1971 when Paulji began to work on me to go on the ECKANKAR Board of Directors, I balked.

I wanted no part of it. But he wasn't bothered by my recalcitrance. When he saw he couldn't budge me head on, he used the back door approach. He told me to attend the meetings so that I would know what things needed to be written up in the publications. Privately, he told board members that I would be coming on the board. When he translated, the existing board had a vacancy, and I was immediately voted on. I remember sitting in my first meeting and having a little private talk with him on the inner: It simply isn't possible to say no to you, is it Paul Twitchell?

I did not particularly enjoy the business of the board, but they made me secretary and I had to learn it well. I often wondered, why am I doing this? Why did Paulji want me here? When my husband died ten years later, and I had to be able to take care of myself in a boardroom, I sent out a silent communication: I guess you must have known I was going to need this, Paulji. Thank you for this gift, my friend.

Fifteen

During the 1960s the world, and particularly the United States, was in a state of social revolution. The Beatles, the rock and roll group from England, were setting trends in music and dress that shocked the conservative, established older generation. The United States was involved in a war in Vietnam which was increasingly unpopular with the people, particularly the younger members of society who were being conscripted to fight it. A mass rebellion against the draft was being staged and was spreading throughout the college campuses. The rebellion was supported by many responsible adults. Timothy Leary introduced LSD — a powerful hallucinogenic drug used previously only in experimentation by intellectuals — to the kid in the street. Minority groups — black, brown, women, the disabled — began to look at the inequities in their lives and believe there was a chance to air their grievances and effect important social changes. John F. Kennedy, an American president who held great appeal for the young and disenfranchised, was assassinated.

Beginning in 1945, there had been a series of atmospheric nuclear tests. The government said they were harmless to the ecology of the planet. The ancient masters, who often serve as a bridge between science and theology, said otherwise. They were concerned about the effect of these tests on the Van Allen belt, a shield of charged particles that encircles the earth's atmosphere. This shield serves as a radiation barrier. Paulji said it also functions as a barrier between the physical-material world, that of solid matter, and the lower Astral Plane, the first (and perhaps least pleasant) area of non-physical existence. He said that once this shield was ruptured, the planet would be inundated with all kinds of psychic phenomena. Man would become surrounded by and attracted to the psi aspect of reality. The man in the street would have access to levels of consciousness and powers heretofore known only to a few. At the time, man had no theology which would furnish him with a code of ethics to govern his use of these powers.

Today, with the current knowledge explosion and advances in the branch of physics known as quantum mechanics, scientists on the cutting edge of knowledge have arrived at a position in which they are forced to shake hands with theology. Most important, the theology they will be turning to must furnish them with a very sophisticated sense of ethics and access to the laws of the invisible worlds.

In this context, Paul Twitchell brought out, in 1965, a modern, Westernized version of the age-old teachings he called ECKANKAR, the Ancient Science of Soul Travel. Although there are about as many ideas of what ECKANKAR really is as there are people who know about it, those of us who were with Paulji in the early phases of his work were given one basic rationale: The orthodox religions are ineffective in dealing with the problems mankind will face in the twenty-first century—rampant psychic powers, and scientific technology that penetrates into the worlds beyond. Modern man will find himself increasingly in need of a guided, systematized means by which he can achieve mastership of his personal universe, protection from outside forces currently beyond his control, and a code of the highest ethics to govern himself as he uses his new technology.

The basis for this system of achieving personal mastership is called ECKANKAR. With ECKANKAR, the individual perfects the art of Soul Travel, leaving the body at will and returning to it with full consciousness of the experiences and wisdom acquired while visiting other planes of existence. All of this is done under the guidance of the Living ECK Master. However, the goal is not to be the eternal student, but to eventually become one's own master.

When Paulji first brought out ECKANKAR,

the idea of out-of-body experiences was practically unknown, except in a few esoteric books. When I first took up the study in 1968, most of us were a little embarrassed by the term *Soul Travel*. It seemed too far out in left field, although we each were in ECKANKAR because we felt it was possible, or realized that in the past we had actually done such a thing without understanding what it was. Some of us—I, for one—told no one what we were doing because it sounded so strange.

But things began to change rapidly. Because of the rampant use of drugs, many people were being jolted out of their bodies through chemistry. Doctors Moody, Kübler-Ross, and others began to come forth with research on near-death experiences. The major universities began to research the subject. Today, almost everybody has heard of the out-of-body experience, and the term *Soul Travel* is more interesting than shocking.

Sometimes as I read and listen to what is happening on the planet these days, I get the feeling that the world is coming around to Paulji's way of thinking. But then I realize that, in reality, the world is coming around to its own way of thinking. Paulji was simply way out in front, preparing the system of high ethics and personal mastership that would be appropriate for many seekers when the world arrived where he was. That was his task, and because—without even knowing what I was doing or how I was doing it—I had Soul Traveled to some inner temple and had read the Shariyat-Ki-Sugmad for twenty-one nights, I, too, became involved in his task.

There were times, as I worked and talked with Paulji, when the overview I have just given occurred to me. When that happened, I would become overwhelmed. And so, I kept that reality a little to the side, a slight distance away from me. Even at that, after a lengthy phone call from him, or as I pored over the three or four letters that arrived from him every day in my mailbox, I would often ask myself, "Why me? Why is he pouring so much of himself out to me? What is really going on here?" I didn't understand. Years after Paulji had translated, I heard a rumor, started by someone who obviously was asking himself the same question, that the truth was that I was Paul Twitchell's mistress. I looked incredulously at the person who told me this and then burst into laughter.

"Well," I said, "if that had been the case, perhaps it would have been a lot easier. Come here and let me show you something."

I took him to my file cabinet and pulled out three bulging folders full of letters, memos, newspaper and magazine clippings, and riffled through them. Everywhere were terse little notes to "Patti" and signed "PT." Nowhere could be found a term of endearment, rarely even a personal word. Sometimes he was taking me to task, sometimes he was explaining something. Sometimes he was giving me instructions on how to write; on how to do a certain book or publication; on how to analyze social, political, economic, spiritual trends; and sometimes he was explaining what he was really doing when he appeared to be doing something else. There were hundreds of articles that I was to read because they either broadened my viewpoint or illuminated some dynamic he was interested in. In all, I believe there are three letters in which he shows some gentle affection for my family and me. One of them is a compliment—the only one I ever received—on a piece of work I did. I treasure it beyond telling.

"I have to make a phone call," I said to the chela who had questioned me about this. "This is absolutely everything Paulji ever sent me. You stay here and go through it and save out all the romantic pieces to show me when I get back." I went upstairs, barely able to control my mirth.

That was the end of that rumor, or at least, that was the last I heard of it. The chela who looked at all my correspondence was not only thoroughly convinced the rumor was ill-conceived, he was stunned at the volume of information Paulji had found time to fire off to me. As other stories have come to me from other people who knew him, and from Gail, I have learned that I was far from the only one who was being bombarded with all these thoughts and letters. The man seems to have been such a vast reservoir that no single individual could have survived being the sole terminal for him. I sometimes felt as if I were holding out a tiny bucket, while an ocean overhead poured itself out on me. With my tiny bucket, I could catch only a very small portion. It staggers me to think that there were quite a few others getting similar outpourings.

The Youth Council held in Las Vegas in March 1971 consisted of a group of about twenty-five people Paulji wished to groom for leadership roles in ECK. In addition to the Youth Council, he hoped to form a large group channel for the positive force, a channel through which some useful, higher consciousness material could enter into the physical world. He knew that it would require a lot of in-depth, personal attention from him if this were to work as he visualized. Three of those who attended are currently members of the Spiritual Council, the council of ECKANKAR's Eighth Initiates; one became Paulji's successor. Some of the other attendees are still with us, working in their home areas. Some have stepped aside and have not been around for quite a while. But at that time, Paulji lavished his attention and his flow of wisdom upon them all.

As a part of his plan, we stayed in the same hotel and worked together all day, and met again in evening sessions. We took every meal together and he always joined us. Each evening after the work was through, as was his custom at seminars, different members of the group were invited up to Paulji's and Gail's room for socializing. For me, this was always the best part. Paulji would have soft drinks and mineral water brought in. Then the folks, usually about ten to fifteen, would sit around and chat.

Paulji was full of good humor and funny stories during these visits. He seemed to be relaxing and enjoying his students. It was only later, when he really started talking to me about his methods, that I began to suspect that in these seemingly light-hearted, social times he was perhaps doing some of his most important work.

In the years since he left this world, I have pondered over what took place during those times. The more I look at it, the more convinced I am that he never did *anything* without a reason; and the more innocuous an action seemed, often the more important was the work going on underneath. Part of his function was to draw off the aberrations or karma of his students. He later told me that sometimes, when it was least expected, through apparent stumbling or laughter, while the chela was off guard, he would use the distraction to pull out a large chunk of the problem or karma the chela was working through. With the chela's attention focused on some outer thing, he or she was completely unaware of what had taken place.

Whatever was going on beneath the surface, these gatherings were great fun. The room would be filled with love and laughter. Indeed, he did seem far happier and more relaxed on these occasions than at any other time I saw him.

I am very grateful for the habit I had gotten into of running my tape recorder whenever Paulji was around, for without these tapes, so much would have been lost. While one is in the moment, it seems that what is going on, being said, thought, or felt will live forever in one. I certainly thought this was true about myself and those times, until I began listening to these tapes in preparation for writing this book. Only then did I realize how much I had forgotten. In addition, I find that things which did not mean anything to me then, now have a significance that I was too busy or too unaware or too noisy to have really understood at the time. Reviewing the tapes has brought these experiences into a sharp focus. I find my memories delightfully revived by the same sound, color, and vibration that was there when it all occurred.

With the use of the tapes and my revived memory, I would like to recreate several scenes from this Youth Council, as they demonstrate Paulji in action, in his various working modes. The first scene is in the meeting room, which was upstairs in the hotel, right across the hall from the casino dealer's lounge. As our spiritual students marched in and out of the meetings, they passed the open door of this lounge where there was a good deal of raucous laughter, cigarette smoke, colorful language, and, fascinating to me, constant card games being played.

In the council room, tables had been set up in a horseshoe pattern, thus enabling the participants to see each other. Paulji addressed the group before the three daily sessions began — the morning, afternoon, and evening sessions. Then he would tell us to get to work, and he would leave. As he talked to us, he sat at the head table, by my tape recorder. He would twist his watchband, then pull his watch off his arm, set it down on the table, pick it up and look at it, then put it back on. He would smooth his hair, rub his face, tug an ear, fiddle with a pencil. His hands were in constant motion. Many of my tapes were all but ruined as he pushed water glasses around, spun and dropped pencils, tapped the table with fingers, pens, or eating utensils. Apparently, the currents flowing through him would not allow him to hold still. Through the magic of the tape recorder and my memory, let's peek in on a portion of the formal session of that Youth Council. Paulji is talking to the group about the most effective ways of teaching. Although he wishes to teach us this method, it is apparent that he is telling the group how he himself works. I have edited the tape for clarity, to make a transition between the spoken and written word, but have tried to retain the Southern flavor and uniqueness of Paulji's personal style.

"You have to remember that when you're out there teaching in the field, you can't give just one level of teaching to the people. You have to be in a position so that what you say to people strikes all levels of consciousness.

[Paulji then pointed to a college professor in the group.] "Now, you know that when you're teaching, you are fortunate if you reach five percent of the students in your class. But, on the other hand, if one has the ability as a teacher to make a statement which hits all levels then practically everybody says, 'Gee, he was talking to me directly. I know it.'"

"Well, this is a phenomenal trick in the teaching field. People have known this thing from Plato down—that is, how to make a statement in which the instructor can touch practically every level of consciousness. It has to do with reaching the individual by using a general trend the instructor knows is running through the group.

"Now, he's fortunate if he can read the collective aura of the group and speak right into this aura, or if he can get the feeling of the group flowing out to him and speak into this feeling area. If he can do this, he can pretty well handle the material for the whole group by making a statement, which will be a general statement, and yet touch all people.

"Anyone who is a student of the Bible or any of the sacred writings, but particularly the Bible which we are more familiar with in this country, knows that not all the statements attributed to Jesus were actually statements that Jesus made, but they were made later by good writers in their translations. They knew that a statement something like, 'Those who are poor in heart shall see me,' [Note: Paulji chronically misquoted the Bible] I believe that's the statement that came out of the Beatitudes—something of that nature—that this would be a statement that would reach a tremendous number of people because all he is saying is that those who are poor in consciousness are so because they are lacking the sophisticated

213

consciousness. And those who do not have the sophisticated consciousness can be reached faster than those who have the sophisticated consciousness. More people can understand that statement and they can leave the room and say, 'Well, gee, he was talking to me,' Each one felt 'he was talking personally to me,' because of a statement of this nature—and these biblical writers knew this.

"Some say that [Matthew, Mark, Luke, and John] did not write these Gospels. They may have written the originals, but the Gospels have been worked over so many times by other writers that they are set in another pattern. [Paulji then gave examples from different versions of the Bible.]

"So, you have people rewriting the King James version, rewriting it until they have perfected it to reach all mankind, all states of consciousness.

"I know that within—oh, fifty years, some of my works will be rewritten in the same form; it's all right, I have no objections. It's like Mary Baker Eddy's works. She met Vivekenanda from the Vedantist Society, and he worked with her on that book about health and science. Later when these people passed away, her own people decided that this wasn't the right sort of thing for Mary Baker Eddy to have in her very famous book, so they rewrote it. And they rewrote it into a common language. So many of these things are done this way. And we have to remember that they were doing the same thing that we were doing in trying to stand up in front of a group, trying to reach them through their own states of consciousness.

"Now, I can say to you, 'Come unto me and I will lift you up.' This is a wonderful statement. This is a statement that will be forever in the minds of people as an inspiring statement. What so many of you do not understand is that no teacher is going out in front of a group and try to lift the whole group up into his level of consciousness in order to talk to them. He has to vary his talk and his statements—he goes down, he goes up and he goes down. If you had a record or a seismograph needle working on the way he was talking in reaching states of consciousness, it would probably go up and down and around, and then straight and then up and then in different areas.

"He'll start his words to one person here, and then he will pitch up to this person and then he will come around to another part of the room, and he sees or feels a flow there, and he'll pitch it down before he even finishes a sentence or a paragraph in his speech. He knows these things, and he is well-versed in this. Now, Plato, I think—I forget which one of his works it was—the one he did on Socrates' death—he did this very well in the sense that he kept pitching his words to reach different states of consciousness.

"I remember several years ago—I think you remember this too, Gail—I got a record out of a public library in Seattle that was done by Professor Moses from Columbia University. He did the whole commentary, the whole running works of Plato on the death of Socrates. And the way this man was pitching this consciousness — do you remember that? He had a marvelous voice and the way he would read this, you could just see it in your mind — like a flash upon the screen that is going up and down, and then way down to a low pitch, and then he'd suddenly come up to a high pitch, even before he'd finished one sentence.

"There was another record that I remember. It was Charles Laughton's talk on the 'Windows of Chartres.' This was the Chartres Cathedral in France; I think it's about twenty-five miles south of Paris. It has the most beautiful windows of any cathedral in Europe. This man, Charles Laughton, had one of the best voices, the best dialogue and diction, that I have ever heard in public. He was an actor who died in [1962]. This man was a marvel, and the way that he could pitch his voice in getting into the state of consciousness of the different groups was absolutely flawless.

"Now, you'll also find this in readings, if you don't gulp the readings. Sometimes the classics bore me, but I think the one that John Keats did upon the Elgin Marbles. . . . do you remember that, anybody? Do you remember what I'm talking about there, any of you others? Anyway . . . no, it's Chapman's Eulogy upon the Elgin Marbles. . . ."

I would like to pause here to blend what was going on in 1971 with something in the present. As I pondered Paulji's apparent confusion about the Elgin Marbles, I decided that I would do some research and get this question answered. Then I was called away from my writing because I had an appointment some miles away. I reluctanctly put down my work and got in my car. How wonderful that I did, for as I drove down the freeway, the question of the Elgin Marbles and Paulji's confusion was still with me. Also with me was my insight from earlier that Paulji had reasons for everything he did.

All of a sudden it dawned on me. When he would stumble, when he would be stuck for a name, a word, or even when he would misquote, he immediately changed the person listening from a position of passive inflow, to an active, thinking participant. I remembered all of us perking up, sitting up in our chairs, thinking very hard about what was the correct answer. It was a very important part of Paulji's philosophy that people need to cease being passive and the effect of things, and become active and cause. Perhaps he didn't plan it this way with his conscious mind, but he certainly did create just such a situation with us, not only with the spoken, but also the written word. But, he was saying something interesting. Let's join him again in his talk.

"The Elgin Marbles are very famous pieces of frieze that came from the Greek Parthenon. They were taken to England and now they are in the National Museum. . . . After Keats saw the Marbles, he wrote this famous poem. It's very musical; it has wonderful lyrics in it. And do you know, he did this same thing within this short poem — it must be about twenty-four lines long — he did the same thing, pitching to the various consciousnesses. He wrote the whole history of ancient Greece within this short poem. It is so visualized in this that you can read the poem and actually get the whole thing — the Trojan Wars and the Greek Mysteries — all of the things which made up the Greek life.

"Now, while I'm on that, you must remember that the Greeks were Oriental in their thinking — probably the first of the Westerners to ever think in the whole. Everyone else thought in parts. And this is the secret and the trick of all of the great people who have been teaching: They would speak into the whole of something, instead of speaking into the part. This is what Keats did in this poem, he spoke in the whole of all the visions that were flashing through his mind — visions of Greek history — and what he learned that night. And he caught this inner vision of the Golden Days of Greece.

"When an instructor wants to put across a point, he speaks in the whole to the group, and the majority of this group will find something in all of this for themselves.

"As I said, the classics always bored me from the time that I was big enough to read them, to the present time, but sometimes I go back and read them. In doing this, I find that they did the same thing: speak in the whole.

"Now, Emily Dickinson, a New England poet — she died in 1886 — was a spinster. After her father died, she spent all of her time within her own home. She never left her home at all. I don't even think that she went to the corner grocery to get things; she always had everything brought in. She never got any farther than her backyard and died as a woman in her middle fifties. Her poems are written in the same form of speaking in the whole. You say, where do these kinds of people get this sort of thing? What happens that they can get a vision of the whole, when we're out here talking to people and haven't even got an inch of it?

"But after a while you catch this thing — and teaching, I think, is the greatest way in the world to get it. I believe the way to learn a subject, whether you already know it or not, is to go out and teach it. And if you teach it, you'll get it. If you don't, it's going to be a hard way to go: trying to study and being the effect of something. You're sitting out there in the audience, listening to somebody, and you're the effect. See?

"This is what made me a poor student in things like algebra or trigonometry or any of these subjects, even history: because I wasn't interested in what the teacher was saying. I was interested in what I could know and learn and find out for myself in researching something.

"There was a time when I was a freshman in high school — I think it was in history — and I wasn't making it, because I wasn't particularly interested in dates and events, and all that sort of thing. But I sat down that one semester and decided that I'd read and study and research and get everything about the Greek athlete that I could. And, you know, I knew more about Greece when I got through reading than I think the professor ever knew about it, because I caught the vision. I caught the background, and I caught the spark of inspiration to find out what it was about, see? If they'd given a test on the Greek athlete, I'd probably have made a triple A.

"Anyway, this is the thing which I'm trying to get across to you tonight: the fact that if you go to this whole and teach and work from this whole idea in your mind — that ECK is the whole thing, out of It springs all religions, all life, everything else — and you teach from this whole, then it goes out and it touches the whole audience. And somebody will pick it up and be sparked by it. They will probably come up some day and have questions that you couldn't even think of answering — because they have gotten a vision on something, and that's their experience. And that's our experience, learning from these people."

Paulji was about to leave when one of the students asked him for the name of Keats's book. With that, he launched into a whole new story about how Keats was buried near Rome in a Protestant cemetery, about the grave of Browning, an anecdote about Thomas Merton, the loneliness of the true spiritual seeker, and more. By the time the group broke up, it was nearing ten at night, but there were the special invitations that had been extended to some to join Paulji in his room afterwards.

220

As I was driving to my appointment this morning, I stumbled upon the insight about Paulji not finding a name or word and asking for help from the audience. I also had some interesting thoughts concerning his teaching us to speak into the consciousness of the audience. Actually, he never really gave more than just what is written on these pages. Some of us got it, and some of us didn't. Again, it is that matter of awakening the vision in one. I learned to do this.

I was thinking about this and how I could explain it so that you, the reader, could catch the vision. It is not an easy thing, as I cannot truly say what it is we do that causes us to read an audience's collective aura and speak or write into it. I know I am not conscious of doing this, but today it occurred to me that it is very much like what I do when I cook a lovely dinner for company. This is the best analogy I can think of:

Before my company comes I try to think about what they like, or if there is no real way to know, I try to make food that I "feel" they will like. I have to work within the seasons and what is fresh and available as I put together my menu. Often, if I am particularly interested in a certain type of cooking at that time, I may plan something that will work in with my interest, because that is obviously where I will have the most energy and attention. And there is usually one thing I plan as a part of the meal that I have never done before. I enjoy doing something new because most often it pleases my friends, and in the process, I learn something too.

I am not sure exactly why, but in my home, the kitchen seems to be the gathering spot or focal point for our guests. I very much enjoy visiting with my guests while cooking, and often as not, I will put them to work. (What was the name of that poem about the Marbles?)

I try, at all times, to practice "conscious cooking"—a method that was once taught me by a Sufi master. Conscious cooking means that every item used is regarded with complete attention and a sense of gratefulness for the gift of itself to us in the meal. In conscious cooking, one is totally here and now. (I am not always completely conscious of every move in my cooking, but it is my goal.) I do always follow the rule that one never cooks a meal when one is angry or upset. I meticulously monitor my emotions when I am preparing food for others.

When we finally sit down to the meal, my guests will most likely say what tastes good and what is a new experience. It has proven itself, over and over again, that I always get more compliments about the deliciousness of a meal that I have cooked totally consciously. For some reason, the food actually tastes better; surely, it must also be better for us.

After the meal is over, it has generally turned out to be a good experience all around. Still, I don't really know if what I cooked was exactly what certain of my guests' cells needed nutritionally that moment or not. I just thought what I thought and cooked what I cooked. Yet, if my cooking works as my lectures and writing do, then somewhere in all that, some precisely correct cell food has been included for someone. It works that way because of Soul's ability to perceive the whole, even while the human part is giving itself other reasons and causes for things. I suppose, however, conscious cooking really works because of what I said early on in this book—because one lets go—and *trusts*.

Sixteen

Paulji is seated next to Gail in the crowded dining room in the Las Vegas hotel. It's lunchtime at the Youth Council. Three other chelas are seated with them, including me and my trusty little tape recorder. For some reason, there are not enough menus to go around. Paulji is holding the one assigned to the Twitchell family, while Gail patiently waits her turn. He is, however, talking to those of us sitting there and is quite engrossed in what he is saying. Finally Gail addresses him. "If you're going to read it upside down, I'm going to take it."

"Oh, I thought that was Chinese." There is laughter from all around the table. "That did look pretty strange, come to think of it."

Still laughing, he hands the upside-down menu to Gail.

"He thought he was in the Fremont Hotel," I interject.

My comment was in reference to a past conversation in which Paulji, knowing that I am fairly gullible, really put me on about the food at the Fremont Hotel. This is a perfect demonstration of how he could kid with a straight face and I'd go for it. Later, I began to watch him more carefully and usually got wise to him quickly. But on that occasion, I fell for it:

"I'll tell you," Paul had said, "if you want a good place to eat, that's the Fremont Hotel. You can get anything you want there."

[Here I take the bait, folks!]

"Downtown?"

"Yeah. They've got Chinese food; you can get Singapore food; you can get Lisbon food; you can get Guinea food."

"All in one *place?*" I ask incredulously.

"Sure. You can get Congo food."

"That sounds like fun." There is a long silence, then my eyes narrow, "Are you putting me on?" Suddenly, I am reduced to giggles. "Gee, I was going to go there."

"You really can get more of a variety of food there than you can get at most places."

"What's Congo food?"

"Boiled boll weevils. Chocolate-covered ants. I could never go for those, but they are supposed to be a delicacy among the jet set."

"Chocolate-covered *ants!* I have enough trouble with snails."

"Spray 'em with chocolate. The kids will eat

226

'em. Good way to get rid of them."

By that time, Paulji was laughing heartily, and I had entirely given up any idea that there would be even the slightest bit of sense to be gotten out of the whole conversation.

Back at the Las Vegas hotel, Gail, having turned the menu right side up, reads it, and then hands it to Paulji.

"Do you remember," she says to him, "when we used to go over to the . . . what was it?"

"Steamboat," Paulji replies.

"Showboat," she says, suddenly reminded. "We played with nickels and quarters and used to come home with *cups* full of coins! We used to have enough to do laundry for weeks . . . all those quarters and nickels."

Paulji turns to me. "What kind of a meeting did you have?"

"Good, really good. A group consciousness is forming, a good flow."

"Now you see what all my conniving does? I sit back there in the little place, twenty-four hours a day, figuring up things for all of you to do."

I look at him and laugh. "I'm aware of that," I say. "I used to believe I was thinking them up myself, but I've got it figured out now."

Paulji is grinning, an undercurrent of mirth bubbling beneath his words.

"I'm sending out messages to all of these

people. They don't know that, though. They think they're figuring it out."

"I used to think up something," I say, "all out of my own head, and then you'd call up about three days later and say, 'You know what I think you ought to do?' and I'd have it half-done or finished, already. Each time I'd think, But *I* thought of that."

We all have gone through the decision-making process and have ordered our food. Now we settle down to a really typical Paul Twitchell lunch conversation. The following conversations are edited for clarity.

Paulji: I saw an interesting thing in the paper the other day. The South has made the first gain in population since the Civil War.

Patti: Really?

Paulji: They made a half million gain in the last two or three years.

Helen: In other words, people are going back into the South now.

Paulji: Well, that's because of the industry. You see, the problem with the deep South has been that nobody would come in to take up industry. But now the New England states and those places which have mills are finding something very different down there. In the North they're contending with the unions. And the next thing that they're contending with is the fact that water is running out in the North, and it takes fifty gallons of water to make one yard of cloth. If they don't get the water, and fresh water especially, which is very abundant in the South, then they're out of luck because the dyes or something don't come out right.

[There is a discussion about mills and mill towns and the Southern plantation owners' treatment of their slaves.]

Paulji: The biggest problem in the South wasn't the plantation owners fighting the issue of slavery as much as it was the Irish. There were a great number of Irish imported into the South at that time because they were hired to do the work on the river levees and roads and everything else; they were common laborers, and they'd make about five to ten dollars a week. If they made fifteen dollars, they thought they were in heaven. So the Irish didn't want these slaves released. If they were, it would ruin their labor market.

Another thing, the fight wasn't really over slavery as much as it was over control. The South, from the beginning—in George Washington's time—from the time that we started this country up until the Civil War, the South was so powerful politically in national affairs that the North got afraid of this, and they decided that the only way out was to start a war and just crush the South. And actually, the fight was against . . .

Someone: . . . power.

Paulji: Yes, the industry of the North versus the slave labor of the South.

Patti: In other words, it really wasn't a moral issue at all.

Paulji: No, it wasn't a moral issue. It's just like the racial issue today. There's nothing in that that makes it a moral issue; it's a power struggle. So many of these things are power struggles. I tried to get that out the other night, about power struggles. And then you begin to get conflicts between the gods, see, like the old mythology thing. Mythology was the conflict between the gods; man made this up to excuse himself.

Patti: I thought that was really good, that even the ECK Masters sometimes throw rocks at each other. There's no hope for peace, Paulji?

Paulji: No. It's just the fact that these people in our time have to get steam off. And to get steam off, it's better for two fellas to go out and throw rocks at one another than to start wars.

Someone: And involve a lot of people.

Paulji: Right. See, they know that.

Patti: In other words, if one doesn't work it off directly in that way, like throwing a rock or something, he'll manipulate others to fight off his aggression for him?

Paulji: Sure.

Patti: Whole nations, perhaps?

Paulji: Well, if you ever get a chance, there's a book to read — it may be in the public library now. The author is Berle [Adolf A. Berle], who just died the other day; I guess he was in his eighties. He wrote a book entitled just *Power*. It came out about two years ago, and it's one of the most fascinating books about fights between powers, every type of power, that you could think of: economic power, religious power, political power. It's about how individuals and groups came up, how they built on power. The real naked power that you have today in the states is actually labor; labor is pure power.

Helen: I guess that would be why the North feared the South, because the South had this cheap labor—this unpaid labor—and the North had to pay for its labor; so, therefore, the South would get wealthier faster and easier than the North could?

Paulji: Well, that was one thing. The other thing was the voting power of the slave states. Now, for example, prior to the Civil War, the whole administrative power of the North and South was all controlled by the Southerners: the Secretary of War, the Secretary of the Navy, all of these people, except President Buchanan, who was from Pennsylvania, were all wrapped up in the South. And the South had the control.

There was a man by the name of—let's see, I'm trying to think of his name now. Anyway, he was a big politician from down in my part of the world who was in Congress at the time, and his wife was the daughter of Senator Ray from Pennsylvania. This fellow that I'm talking about was from the South, from Tennessee; he was the majority whip of Congress. He eventually married Ann Ray from Pennsylvania, whose father was the leading senator in Congress, and her cousin was Millard Fillmore, who was from Buffalo, New York, or some place up in there. Before they married, this congressman was writing letters to his fiancée, and it was a very interesting thing. I've seen these letters, and these letters talked about all the problems that were coming, the coming political storm, and how they could never settle on anything because of the Southern block.

When Polk was in there, in 1846, as the president, there was a great problem. He wanted to, and he did, start a war with Mexico in order to gain Texas and make that a Southern state. There was opposition because if he brought in the biggest state in the union, the North knew that the Southerners would have complete control. Well, instead of only bringing in Texas, he brought in the whole southwest territory.

The same kind of fight is going on today in Congress that was going on then; because somebody was gaining too much control—and that was the South—which brought on the War between the States.

Patti: I'd like to read this book, *Power*. It sounds interesting. What's the man's last name, Paulji?

Paulji: Berle. This man had a very fine background. In 1933, he was an economic advisor in FDR's "brain trust." He has a wonderful grasp of history and power—how it all is made. He was also at Columbia University for many years. He taught law and history, and a lot of things like that.

Patti: You know, you were saying something about the basic things that push man—I can't remember how you put it. Self-assertion was one of them. Was power the other one?

Paulji: Determination. And then there's motivation. Rather, the motivation starts it and then you have . . .

Patti: Doesn't he need the power to assert himself? Is that what the power is behind most of the . . . ?

Paulji: Well, let's take the case of Al Capone. Al Capone was nothing but just a modern highway robber, see? He knew how to appear to work within the law but also how to use his guns; he was a power unit. Then he'd always have to battle rival gangs all the time. Frankly, no man ever stays in the position of power very long because power is destructive.

Helen: And it destroys the man that's using it.

Paulji: Right. I think most of the presidents of the United States within the past fifty or hundred years have realized this: that destruction comes with power.

Patti: Is it that absolute power corrupts absolutely?

Paulji: Yes, right.

Helen: Rebazar Tarzs talks about power, wisdom, and freedom.

Paulji: He's talking about a different thing. Now, there's a very interesting thing in all of this—this power thing—this power structure on earth. Let's go back to the time of Jesus. You see, the Romans were the absolute power. And by being the absolute power, they were always

233

watchful of someone else who they thought would erode their power or would be an influence of rebellion. . . . In the Middle East, they had patrols. These patrols were always out watching, and they constantly had spies. If they caught anybody at all who they believed was raising any point of rebellion, they had them — through the spies.

There was a very interesting book by Vardis Fisher, *Jesus Came Again: A Parable,* about the power structure. He wrote it in a fiction story about this fellow who lived a hundred years after Christ. He was nothing but a beggar wandering around on the roads. One day he picked up a slave girl who had a sick baby, and while in his presence, this baby got well. Due to the ignorance of her mind and her slavery, the mother said her baby was healed by this fellow. And this was one thing that the Roman authorities were against, because when they got any crowds or anything around one man they seized him; the patrols went out, seized the guy, and brought him in.

So this poor guy was wandering around, and he was trying to dodge all of this fame, because he knew the problems that would come. He'd go someplace to sit down, just to rest, and a whole group of people would get around him. His reputation followed him. He knew that one of the fellows that took up with him was a Roman spy. So what did he do? He got in this crowd in the marketplace one day, determined to hide himself and somebody discovered him; so they all started gathering around him, and he kept saying, "I'm

234

not all of this, I'm not all of this." And there was this dippy slave woman back there saying, "He is too; he healed my baby!" Of course, the spy took off to report him, and in a few minutes the patrol was there and picked him up. This guy had known what was going to happen, because the gathering of crowds around a man like him was a point of rebellion that the Roman authorities were afraid would someday usurp the power.

Patti: Which is what happened.

Paulji: Yes. And, you see, Constantine did the same thing in 325. He went through the same process and decided to accept Christianity because it had a pretty strong hold on his people. By accepting Christianity, he could keep his empire together.

The two sects within Christianity were having a big fight. One was more powerful, and Constantine banished the lesser one to Egypt. He told the less powerful sect to go there and not bother him anymore.

There was a lot more, but I think you get the idea. All through this discourse lunch was served and eaten, and Paulji somehow managed both to eat and follow these fascinating trails inside his mind.

Seventeen

At the Youth Council in Las Vegas in March 1971, Paulji spoke several times a day to the group of students. As previously mentioned, he also took his meals with the group in the hotel dining room. I have given samples taken from the tapes of his work with the formal group, and of a typical lunch conversation in which his mind soared through history, book reviews, and several dynamics, mainly that of power.

At around ten-thirty in the evening, after he gave his last talk of the day to the group in the formal session, he would go to his room. There he would entertain a smaller group which he had invited to visit with him. These late-evening sessions took place at every seminar. While they were easy and fun, and while he always seemed relaxed and humorous, there is no doubt that they were just another way of teaching. These late-evening sessions were filled with stories and anecdotes. I suspect that many — if not all of them — were parables.

Paulji always had a sitting room or another room in addition to his sleeping room. He said that people brought him such problems that the room in which he had met them vibrated with those problems long after they had left. By the time he had done four or five of these consultations in a day, he found that he couldn't sleep at all if he was in the same room where they had taken place.

Singly, or in pairs, those invited to his after-hours sessions would knock on the door and be admitted to this sitting room by whoever of the staff got there first.

Usually, before any of us arrived, he would have arranged with room service for a variety of soft drinks, tonics, and mineral water, with plenty of glasses. Each guest, upon arrival, was offered a cool, refreshing drink. This was especially important and appreciated in Las Vegas, where the humidity is very low and people tend to get parched.

Paulji would be seated in a comfortable chair, and as each guest arrived, he greeted him or her enthusiastically and asked about something personal: work, hobbies, children, etc. He seemed to retain an extraordinary amount of personal information about each of our private lives, right down to the names of spouses and their occupations, and the names and ages of our children. This may not *seem* extraordinary, but the sheer numbers made it so. While any single evening might find a dozen to a dozen and a half people in his room, they were not always the *same* people. I believe the chelas who were treated to this special experience with him would add up into the hundreds.

Generally, Paulji talked for a little while about any seminars coming up and, in between little snippets of business, he would kid around with people. Both he and his visitors would tell funny stories that would have the whole room laughing. Then, as people laughed and relaxed, he would casually change the subject. While it seemed he was simply blending in another funny story with the light-hearted bantering, he would slip in something that was very definitely meant to be instructive.

An example of one of these sudden shifts of gears is the evening that Paulji began to relate a recent incident in which a woman at a seminar had insisted on annointing his feet with oil. Although he told it in his usual anecdotal manner of gentle, wry humor, it was clear that he had gotten himself trapped into this situation through the woman's persistence, and he had been embarrassed and acutely uncomfortable about the matter. In fact, he said that the whole incident so completely unnerved him that when the staff came to pick him up about thirty minutes later, he was still so distracted about it, he went off and forgot to pay his hotel bill. He said he got all the way home, reached in his pocket and found his room key. He then had to call the hotel to say he'd forgotten to check out.

Although, in its way and in his telling of it, it was a rather humorous story, Paulji was making an important point to the group: If you people are sincere in your desire to be leaders and teachers in ECK, you had better be very clear about the fact that there is no place in ECKANKAR for this kind of thinking and worship in regards to me. It was part of his method: If a chela is told a truth in one sentence, he will forget it by the next morning. If it is told to him in a story or a parable, he'll remember it all his life.

The same evening that Paulji told this story, he engaged in some very funny conversational bantering with Millie Moore—one of his earliest chelas, and one of the prime reasons ECKANKAR was originally headquartered in Las Vegas. People have endlessly conjectured about the significance of ECKANKAR's first international headquarters being in such an oddly disparate location as Las Vegas. As Millie has often explained, Paulji had a bookkeeper—her—a secretary (both of them chelas who happened to live in Las Vegas) and he had Elmo De Whitt, a CPA, who, with his wife, Dorothy, resided in Reno, Nevada. These people could begin the business organization for him— so that's where he incorporated. If some people choose to make something more esoteric and significant about this, it's their privilege, but that is the reason the first ECK office was located in Las Vegas. Back in those early days, Millie and the secretary used to haul all the chela records and the financial books of ECKANKAR around in the trunks of their cars. It is quite a contrast from those times to the large building and huge mainframe computer of today's ECKANKAR.

There were other discussions and funny stories told that evening; then there was a slight, almost imperceptible pause, and suddenly I spoke up.

"Well, Paulji, I think we ought to take off."

"All right. Okay."

"You must be tired," I said. "I know all the rest of us are too."

"Well, all right," he said again.

Before we left, he said he would tell us one more funny story, which he did. Ending on laughter, we said our good-byes and quickly departed.

What happened there at the end of the meeting, when I suddenly said I thought we should take off, was another interesting phenomenon that happened between Paulji and me. I do not know how it started, or when or even how I ever knew it, but at one of these evening socials I got a strong inner signal that Paulji was very tired. When I mentioned the late hour he was very grateful for my noticing. After that, it was a regular occurrence. I think he was probably telegraphing a cue to me, and I would pick it up and gently suggest to the others that it was time to go. If one would read the transcript of this tape, there is an almost tangible message that can be felt right before I say, "Well, Paulji, I think we ought to take off."

It was so subtly done that I feel sure if any of those who had attended these meetings were questioned, none of them would even recall exactly how they ended, but the meetings always came to a close like that.

In the week following the Las Vegas council, I was back down in Del Mar with Paulji, business as usual. My work with Paulji seemed to follow a peculiar rhythm. A difficult assignment, something new and never done by us (or by anyone else in ECKANKAR) would be set up. There would be a corresponding amount of low-key (sometimes not so low) anxiety as to just how and what we would do to accomplish it. Meetings to plan agendas for sessions would be held. Ideas would be batted around, some eventually worked and formed into the nucleus of the project. Other ideas, some of them very good, would be discarded. Later it would be found that they had actually jumped in ahead of their time and belonged to some future event.

The planning was in flux right up to the moment of the event because that seems to be the way of the ECK. Energy, excitement, and work steadily built to a crescendo, culminating in the event itself. I often told myself, if I can only get through this, then things will calm down, and I will be able to get to some of the tasks I've left undone. Following the event, there would be a brief denouement, an analysis of the feedback, and a thoughtful assessment of the project's success. (I don't really remember a failure.) One would almost begin to think it was going to calm down and—zap! Paulji would come up with the next idea, and the whole process would gear up again.

Following the Youth Council, we didn't even get the usual lull. There seemed to be a glitch in the schedule for the seminars to be held around Easter, in April 1971. Paulji was due to attend a seminar in Chicago, which ultimately became the traditional ECKANKAR Youth Conference. About the same time, he was also to attend one in Vancouver, B.C., Canada. Apparently, he had reflected upon the closeness of the two dates and had made a decision, which he decided not to disclose to anyone until the Las Vegas Council was over.

The decision he made really shocked me. He had rescheduled the Vancouver seminar for the same weekend—Easter—as the one in Chicago. He assigned Helen, me, and two or three other High Initiates to run the Vancouver seminar, to be the guest speakers and, in effect, stand in for him. He would be at the one in Chicago.

Today, to be given such a responsibility would be like water rolling off a duck's back. But in April 1971, a regional seminar without Paulji was unheard of. It had never been done. There was deep concern on my part about what the Canadian chelas would have to say about Paulji's absence, and how they would respond to us as stand-ins. We were in a fair state of uncertainty, but we bit the bullet, as we always did when Paulji asked us to do something. This situation did have its exciting aspects: history was being made. And Paulji, with his inner clock ticking away, was weaning us—and the whole movement—away from always needing him to be at all ECK seminars in person.

My memories of that Canadian Easter are a wonderful collage of impressions. Being a southern California girl, and not well-traveled, I didn't realize how different the weather would be; I didn't take a coat. Fortunately, Helen had a spare, because it snowed on Easter Sunday. The seminar was held in the charming, old Vancouver Hotel. The meeting room was furbished with ivory-painted Louis Quinze woodwork and, in contrast to the garish reds of most of the Las Vegas seminar rooms, seemed very gracious and continental.

The Vancouver chelas had somehow procured, literally, buckets of daffodils (coincidently, my favorite flower) and these buckets lined the stage. There must have been thousands of daffodils. I remember how joyous the chelas seemed to be, and how contagious the joy was. The program went quite well, I think, and the Canadians were marvelous. I still have many cherished friendships that began that Easter weekend.

My only other recollection of that seminar is of a talk I gave one afternoon. I asked the ECK to please just make it good enough so the chelas wouldn't be too sorry Paulji hadn't come. I remember feeling quite blank as I stepped out on the stage, and saw the daffodils and all the smiling, friendly faces in the lovely room. Feeling a little anxious, I began to talk. I don't remember what I talked about, but I do remember feeling Paulji's presence so strongly that I wouldn't have been surprised to turn around and see him. Only once did I actually think objectively about what I was doing, and then it seemed, oddly, that I was speaking with somewhat of a Southern accent — or perhaps I imagined it.

Later, some people who had been in the audience told me that they could actually see flickers of Paulji in my face, and that, indeed, I had spoken in a very rich Southern accent, exactly like his. Well, I didn't understand that; I still don't. Later I mentioned to Paulji in a letter what had happened at the seminar. He returned it to me with many marginal notations around my various comments. Next to my report of my talk and the strange, Southern accent, he made the note, "This has put you in line for your next initiation." Somehow, in the busy hustle and bustle of my life, I had managed to forget he had said this. At least, I thought I had.

As soon as Paulji had finished breaking new ground for ECK seminars in Canada, he was on to the next thing. Originally, his schedule for 1971 went like this:

Los Angeles, California	January 22–24
New York, New York	February 19–22
Vancouver, B.C. (Changed to April 9–11)	March 26–28
Chicago, Illinois	April 9–11
Lisbon, Portugal	May 14–17
London, England	May 18–23

245

Chicago, Illinois	June 25–27
(Second International Youth Conference)	
Toronto, Ontario	July 9–10
Cincinnati, Ohio	September 16–19
Las Vegas, Nevada	October 21–24
(Fifth World Wide)	
Dallas, Texas	December 12–14

Of course, like everything else he did, this schedule was subject to change. He had added the Youth Council in early March, and after we returned from Vancouver, he asked us to plan a few training sessions for the Second International Youth Conference in Chicago, in June. After that, he asked for a two-day training session of the young people who lived on the West Coast. This would be in July, in Long Beach, California. However, these events seemed to come like ocean waves, one building upon the other; they were not long-range plans.

That April, an incident occurred in which Paulji's peculiar (at least to most of us) sleep habits came into play. Here on tape, he talks about his sleeping patterns. The text is edited for clarity.

"Gail has to have all the shades pulled down when she goes to bed, and it has to be pitch dark before she sleeps. I'm just the opposite. I have to have a light on and all the shades pulled up. If I don't have the light on, I must have light from someplace else. This is one of the reasons why I often stay up all night.

"I may read or work until midnight. Then I will pick up something light to read and might read the rest of the night until the light comes in at five o'clock in the morning. As soon as it starts getting light, I turn out all of the lights and go to sleep, but I will not sleep in the dark under any circumstances.

"Now, this has occurred ever since I can remember, since I was old enough to have any memory. I had to have a light on in the house, a bed light furnished to me. And, it's a fact that if the full moon is out, then I may go to bed, because I can sleep if there's a light outside. But if it's dark between full moons, I don't make it."

What Paulji didn't cover in the above story was that he would go to sleep about five in the morning and sleep until about nine or nine-thirty. That apparently was all the sleep he required.

Paulji's unusual nocturnal habits created something of a crisis in their new Del Mar house. Having moved from an apartment to a single residence was overall a pleasure for the Twitchells, but there were some of the standard homeowner headaches. The one that caused the most friction in the Twitchell house was the issue of having the lawns mowed. I was at more than one work session with Paulji when the gardener fired up the power mower right next to the window where we were working, and it was absolutely impossible for us to hear each other, let alone tape anything.

Paulji requested that Gail change the day that this power mower came to visit. Gail evidently had requested a different day, but the only time the man had available was at 7:30 in the morning. The first time the mower fired up at 7:30, it created quite an uproar inside the house. Since Paulji only slept four to four-and-a-half hours, this meant he lost half of his night's sleep. He complained to Gail, but she couldn't do much about the gardener's schedule. I think the gardener awoke Paulji again the following week, but never again after that. The next time the gardener was due, a small weather front, carrying little moisture, suddenly escalated into a ferocious storm, making it impossible for the gardener to work that day. Paulji, laughing, told me about it on the phone. He said Gail looked at him in disgust as the winds and rains raged and said, "Don't you think that's overdoing it a bit?"

A few days later, a letter came in my mail. It contained an article cut out of the *San Diego Union,* dated April 15, 1971. The headline read, "Storm Surprises Area, With Rain, Snow, Twister."

Here are a few excerpts from the article.

> A storm that was expected to bring only sprinkles here escalated yesterday into a soaking rain, snow and a mini-tornado. . . .
>
> The San Diego County Agricultural Department said the rain would benefit cattle-grazing land, and should help sustain the perennial grasses planted in the areas burned over in last fall's massive brush fires.
>
> On Mt. Laguna, where the temperature range was thirty-two to forty-four degrees, snow fell

for about five hours. But it has all melted. "We had a high temperature of seventy degrees on Tuesday, so the ground was still warm," said Mrs. Dotti Haak, the weather observer there.

Up to a half-inch of snow fell on Palomar Mountain. That, too, is mostly gone. There were flurries in Cuyamaca State Park, and hail in Julian.

Offshore, a number of funnel clouds were sighted. These are tubular columns of unstable air that churn their way down from clouds. When they touch water, they create waterspouts. When they touch land, they become tornadoes.

One funnel came ashore in Chula Vista, ripping shingles . . . and blowing down a . . . fence. It also whirled through the 1600 block of Melrose Avenue and other sections.

With the storm gone, temperatures are expected to rise today and tomorrow. . . .

Stapled to the article was Paulji's cover letter to me, which made me roar with laughter.

Patti:

Here's the clipping on the storm and story —

Rest I told you on telephone.

Gail was quite annoyed, but I got my sleep —

PT

Eighteen

For the last month, as I have been approaching writing about this segment of my experience with Paulji, I have been suffering a great deal of neck pain and muscle spasm. It is somewhat odd, since I have been completely free of them for almost ten years. It is almost as if, knowing this part was coming, my body's cells and nervous system began remembering the incident that had caused them, even before my brain was ready to approach the subject.

Sometime in April 1971, Paulji sent me a copy of a typewritten letter he had written to a Higher Initiate, who was also a doctor, in which he asked him to raise four people to the Sixth Initiation whenever it was convenient for him. My name was in the letter. At the bottom, in his own handwriting, Paulji had made a note to me: "Patti: This for your info only, to have for publication when events occur—"

It had not quite been a year since I had been given my Fifth Initiation. One day when Paulji called, I said something about this letter and remarked about how fast he was taking me.

"Well," he said, as if this should put an end to any insecurity I might feel about the subject, "Rebazar Tarzs put me through *ten* in *one* year." His tone conveyed the idea, "What's your problem? If I could do that—you can do this!" It was one of the few times he left me speechless.

About a month later, on the fifth of May, I had an appointment to see this particular doctor, for treatment of chronic neck pain caused by two whiplashes many years before. It was decided that while I was there, I would be given my Sixth Initiation and also be served the usual, delicious lunch that the doctor and his wife liked to make for me.

First, Doc worked on my neck, then he attended to the ECK initiation. Afterwards, we relaxed at the dining room table with a wonderful meal. When we had finished eating, the doctor's wife, also a Higher Initiate, became serious. She said, "You know, Patti, sometimes we worry about you. Paul is putting you through these initiations so fast." I shrugged. "I seem to have done fine, so far," I said in a voice that spoke with more confidence than I really felt at that moment.

The drive home was a long one, and I had plenty of time to think. I was not long on the road before a wave of anxiety swept over me. My gosh, these people were some of Paulji's oldest chelas.

I considered them wise and so far beyond me spiritually that I knew I would never catch up. I had honestly never been afraid for myself for even one moment—my trust in Paulji was absolute. But now, here was this concern for me coming from what seemed to be such spiritual giants. Suddenly, for the first time, I began to feel scared for myself. Did Paulji really know what he was doing? They certainly knew him better than I, and they were worried.

I don't really remember how much of the drive I spent in this mild state of panic, but it wasn't too long. I remember feeling this anxiety and then, abruptly, a question posed itself to my mind: What do you *know* in the deepest part of you? I answered without hesitation: I know that I have never gone wrong when I've put my faith and trust in Paulji. In that moment, I knew I was all right. I couldn't figure out how these two Higher Initiates could have less trust in Paulji than I did. Even though they were my most respected authority figures, next to Paulji, I elected to ignore what they had to say and trust my own inner guidance. It was a breakthrough of major significance and really a test. Before I arrived home, I was laughing and inwardly thanking them for being the vehicles for this realization. In that one drive, I finally conquered a long-standing attitude about authority figures. The name of that discolored piece of lens is: *People who have risen to the top of a field know everything there is to know about it.*

The next day, I received from Paulji a copy of a

letter that he had written to the doctor and his wife. Apparently he had written this letter the same day I got my initiation. Paulji was, as they say, on a tear; he was annoyed about something. The following is excerpted from that May 5 letter to them.

Some time ago I wrote you a letter stating that a number of people so named in the letter were to be pulled up from the Fifth Initiation to the Sixth, etc.

I want you to hold up on these initiations until further notice.

I am freezing all initiations from the Fifth upward until some points have been gotten across to the Higher Initiates.

For example, I have definitely made the point about smoking and about complaints. I lectured on the latter subject in Los Angeles, wrote two strong letters in the *ECK Monthly Letter* recently, but it seems few people are paying any attention to what I am saying. I said very clearly, "When any ECKist makes a complaint about a fellow chela, regardless of who or what he might be, he creates a problem for all concerned. And I do not like to have such complaints brought to me because I have to do something about the ones complained against, or the one who is making the complaint. Besides this, those who complain only make greater karmic ties with the ones they complain about . . ."

This also goes for smoking. Those who smoke can at least keep from doing so in front of other chelas. . . . Certain chelas who are doing this are not to be given any more initiations, and are in danger of losing what they have already.

I do not feel that you should get yourselves involved in the youth situation in the Midwest. Frankly, this is all very subtle, but [there is] strong pressure from certain sources upon me to step into the situation, but I steadfastly refuse to do so. So far it isn't any of my affair until those involved in it ask me to do so. When those making the complaints become aware of what is happening to themselves, that their own actions are pulling them down instead of upward, that they are victims of Krodha, a very useful servant of the negative power, they will stop it. . . . They could all cause a loss in whatever initiation degree that each has, and have to start all over again from the bottom.

It is a local problem and doesn't belong in my province until the concerned, the doers themselves, ask me about it.

At this point I am not going to give any more initiations on the higher levels until such complaints are halted, as well as other practices. I have said this again and again, but few seem to pay any attention to what is being said.

I mean no harm to anyone, but it certainly is disturbing to have to listen to all this sort of thing going on constantly among the chelas, the Mahdis, Shabbas [sic], etc.

My love to you both, and please spread the word on this to others on these points.

Affectionately,

Paul

Written in black felt-tip pen along the border was a marginal notation to me: "Patti—this is becoming a bore and an amusing thing—PT"

Well, needless to say, it was not an amusing thing to me. I pretty much became unglued. I really had no idea what had triggered Paul's stern letter, but I knew it was some issue in the Midwest, and that I was not guilty of either smoking or complaining. What really bothered me was that even as I was being initiated, he was putting a blanket freeze on initiations. Immediately, I sat down and fired off a note to him.

> Paulji—
> Doc gave me Sixth yesterday—Today I received your letter to them—Wow—Am pretty shook. Do not understand how he could make a mistake like this—
>
> > Patti

The next day Paulji called before my letter had had a chance to reach him. I blurted out what had occurred. He was very quiet, as if processing what had taken place. I thought he was, perhaps, mildly amused, but he only said, "Don't worry about it." I have a handwritten copy of a letter I wrote to him the next day. I do not know if I later typed it, or if I ever sent it at all.

> Sat—May 8
>
> Dear Paulji:
> I was so glad to talk to you yesterday and hear your words about the initiation. Funny thing about that. At one level I was unperturbed—even a bit amused—but that was the part of me

that laughs at anything that goes on here—and at myself, when I get too serious about it all. But, then, on the other level, I really was upset, for I take nothing in ECK lightly.

It was all like musical chairs—and I got the last chair before the music stopped. One has to wonder about the timing of such things. If I were counseling one of the chelas on such a thing, I'd be telling them it was meant to be.

I have several points to bring up though. First, I hope you understood what I meant when I said, "It didn't matter." I reasoned that if Doc had made a mistake and you wished to remove the initiation or whatever, how would I take it? And I knew that wherever I am, it is the right place. I can accept anything, particularly if you think it is best.

I know it is an honor—but an honor in the world—those things are not important to me. It is my INNER HONORS, joy and knowing, that I treasure, and they—or I—am that, regardless.

The second thing, if you wish this not to be known in order for your disciplinary points to be more effective, or whatever, we can keep it quiet. A few in my group know—and Doc—that's all. If I tell them, they'll never say a word.

It surely was something new in initiations for me. No lights and gongs and Cecil B. DeMille—a strange tugging, like I wasn't running to it, but dragging my feet a bit (typical attitude the last few weeks). What is that last little thing that hangs on to us? Or we to it? Lord, I should have thought there was nothing left to give up. But there was. And I could feel this gentle, little tugging—such a mild experience—yet at Soul

257

level, it was very much like dying (at least Soul's view of it). Such a BIG DEAL to a human, but for Soul, just the same after as before. Finally the human gave up, said, "Okay, you've got it all now. I'm ready to give it all up." And I sat there waiting for the great celestial choir to sing, the blinding flash of Cosmic Light (at least!). But all remained as it was: Simple. Quiet. In balance.

And the searchlight of my attention was directed to a thing I had heard about Milarepa: what a simple, quiet, ordinary-sounding man. And I knew a new thing: *It is all part of me*. At that moment, a bird outside the window began to sing — two beautiful, long trills. The inner voice said, "Even this . . . is you!" And both Doc and I opened our eyes simultaneously.

You know, Paulji, it's a very lovely thing to realize that a bird's song IS a great celestial choir. In fact, in retrospect, C.B. DeMille could never have been profound enough simply to film and record a little bird singing.

Thank you for all. *I am!*

Patti

A flurry of letters arrived in the mail all on the same day. The first one I opened was my letter saying I was pretty shook and didn't know how Doc could have made such a mistake about my initiation. Paulji had scrawled a note at the bottom which trailed up the right margin: "Okay you're in — by a narrow squeeze — We're only saving 200 Souls this year — You were head of list — so enjoy trying on your halo and wings — PT"

Another came — again handwritten — in his bold felt-tipped, half-cursive, half-printed writing.

Patti:

I said the other day the word was "Shaddha" for Sixth Initiates — but it's really "Shradda" — the next printing of initiation brochure shall be corrected.

Congratulations — You've made it into the Shraddha Circle and now been saved — not by the bell, but by the flip of the Angel's wing —

PT

Paulji had sent a third letter.

Patti:

If I didn't tell you, the Sixth Initiate is known as the "Shraddha"

I gave you the wrong spelling the other day —

PT

The notes were all I needed to be completely reassured, and I gave no further thought to all the confusion surrounding the incident (including the spelling of Shraddha).

Paulji and Gail took off for Portugal and then England, and I was kind of glad. I was feeling a little exhausted and knew I could use the rest. While they were gone, I made a special trip of my own down to their house in Del Mar and planted a small night-blooming jasmine bush under the window of Paulji's room. It was only with such tiny acts of thoughtfulness that I felt I could ever express to him my gratitude.

Nineteen

Memorandum

To: Paulji
From: Patti
Date: 5/25/71
Re: This week

Dear Paulji:

Debated as things have gone along whether to send you what is happening, blow by blow, or save it all for one big blob. Since much takes care of itself along the way, I opted for one communication.

I tentatively have a title for the new biography, subject to approval. I am not exactly speeding along on this. This change in printers has eaten a lot into my time. I think it will get better, but it is taking more time right now as they just do not know how to do it.

It is hard to explain but it takes a lot of time just to realize what knowledge another does not possess. They have two years of past issues to go over; still they make mistakes. I had a hunch I'd better go over there and check things out the morning they went to press. They had run 2,000 wrong. Did I tell you this? I will just have to see final proofs, and at the rate they are doing it now, I will have to start another week earlier and make more trips.

Everyone is trying super hard too . . . it just takes time, that precious commodity.

I found out that the new copyreader was only on the job one week when he got hit with me and that first eight-page *Monthly Letter*. He is a perfectionist and a nervous type anyway, and is shuddering to think of running off the *Mystic World* and the *Monthly Letter* both in the same month. I am giving it to him early too, but if it is too much of a hassle, I think the better thing to do would be to keep the *Mystic World* with your printer in Chula Vista. I am understanding with people and patient, but do feel that I do not have forever to play around with them while they learn on the job . . . so I have given them a time limit in my mind and then ZAP.

I will run "The Littlest African ECKists" picture in the *Mystic World*. Also would like a statement from you regarding your European visit . . . any observations and comments to make?

Regarding the training program in the Midwest (Youth Conference in Chicago in June): I think I had better hear from you what it is I am to do there.

I seem to be working out an area of awareness in which several individuals disagree with my subjective viewpoint so strongly that I am overpowered, and I begin to doubt my own sanity — that is to say, our subjective viewpoints are so different that it is hard to believe we are talking about the same event.

An example occurred at lunch one day with a Higher Initiate, the doctor's wife. I was telling her about the first time I met you — how I walked up to your table in the coffee shop at the International Hotel and stammered out my name ... I was remembering the coffee shop and myself sitting there for an eternity, trying to screw up enough courage to walk those twenty or so steps. After I told this, she said very indignantly, "THAT IS NOT HOW IT HAPPENED AT ALL!" And she told a story of how the two of us had been talking at a desk when you walked up behind us, after which she introduced me to you. She insisted that it happened like this, and that it was I who did not remember how I first met you. When I tried to suggest that I would not forget this occasion, she got very upset, worrying about how to resolve her mistaken notion. She said, "You must have — I've told this story to many classes." I got to thinking about it and decided, "Well, maybe that's how it happened, and it is I who have thought it to be another way ... I finally agreed it was possible that she was right and I had just forgotten.

263

Now, Paulji, in secret, I still believe that the first time we spoke was in that coffee shop . . . but the point is, I do have a tiny doubt. I am not sure whether it is a vice or a virtue when someone's will is so strong that they can make me question even such a fantastic and memorable experience as the darshan because they are more sure than I, or stronger, or louder, or ? Maybe this is the lesson the ECK has for me right now; I have not solved it completely. I only keep remembering that every time I have been 100% sure about something, I get knocked on my end.

* * *

This last subject in my letter to Paulji is very typical of some of the testing and lessons I was put through in my time with him. While the earlier lessons were quite obvious in what they were about, the honing of my spiritual self was becoming much more subtle now.

Paulji kept assigning me to work with people whose personalities and willpowers were far stronger than mine. If I reached into my inner recesses and pulled out a plan, someone else had a different one they preferred. If Paulji had specifically asked me to work on the project, this put me between a rock and a hard place. My innate tendency was to simply defer to the stronger person. It was more or less an attitude of, well, whoever has the most energy should do the job. I found it very difficult, however, to take this path of least resistance and honor my commitment to Paulji. It seemed unlikely that he would assign me to a project so that I would have the experience of doing nothing because a stronger personality overpowered me.

I was far enough along in my journey to recognize a setup when I saw one. If it happens again and again, there is usually something that is to be learned. If it's upsetting and unpleasant, we seem to learn faster. At least I do. It was one of Paulji's favorite axioms: GROWTH IS IN THE HASSLE.

I do suppose that the discomfort of the experience reached its zenith when the Higher Initiate told me in no uncertain terms what my personal experience had been in my initial meeting with Paulji. The color of this lens is: *I am vulnerable to the ideas and energies of others in determining the truth of my own reality*.

My writing to Paulji about the experience and saying, "I still believe my own version," was the end of that testing. But I saw an interesting thing in the Higher Initiate's certainty about my experience. Someone had taken the most important thing that had ever happened to me — something I remembered in every vivid detail of sight, sound, and feeling — and said it didn't happen that way. I probably have never been so certain of anything in my life, and yet, because of *her* energy, I actually began to have a doubt. If a strong personality can do this to our most powerful experience, what are people out there doing to our realities in normal circumstances?

In order to rid myself of this colored lens, I had to regroup and establish a new approach to such overwhelming strength in others. If I had an idea and someone stronger had a different idea, I would feel fine if I could just have mine heard. If the stronger person insisted on having it his way, I would defer. After all, my task is not to prevail over others, it is merely to channel my work and let it be. If others had a need to prevail, then I was happy to allow them to. But I looked at it then, and still do, as a thing apart from my own reality. No longer can a strong personality compromise what I know to be true within me. However, they may often prevail in my outer world.

The two Higher Initiates, the doctor and his wife, have both translated now, but I owe a tender debt to both of them, for they were the instruments of some of my most profound realizations.

We went on to do the Youth Conference in Chicago, and it all went very well. During this last period of his earthly life, Paulji was increasingly interested in the younger generation. He began to hold many meetings strictly for them and was in the process of a set of discourses for them entitled *Letters to a Chela,* in which he hoped to give them a broader understanding of the world's religions, etc., so that the youth would understand how these religions fit in with the whole, the ECK. The young adults, ages sixteen through thirty, were the people he was giving most of his attention to. They were always working on projects, talking about ECK. And he felt that since they were determined to do that, he wanted them to be well-informed about what other people believed, so that they could understand others and be able to hold intelligent conversations with them.

While the main program was going on at the Youth Conference in Chicago, the age group mentioned above met in a separate meeting room and was treated to several surprise visits from Paulji. At our first youth session, we had people all over the room say their names and then tell something about themselves. Then Paulji walked in. He and several initiates, including Gail, told the young people what part ECK played in their lives. Here's an edited transcript of what was said.

Gail: I guess I've been with ECK, in some ways, since the beginning of time, and I'm happy with Paul and with ECK people. My favorite book is *Stranger by the River*.

Paulji: Do you know, the first time I ever took Gail out, I took her to a pizza house? We sat and talked about this [ECK]. She went home thinking this guy was crazy. And I think about the fifth time we went out, there was an automobile with a couple of rough-looking characters and a girl in it. They were coming up this way [he gestured with his hands] and they kept blocking my way. I wanted to make a left turn and so I thought I'd bluff 'em. I pulled towards 'em and they ripped over to the side and back and then they pulled in front of me and started to stop. Of course, my heart went up to right about here. [He pointed to his throat.] I think the girl must have said

267

something to them because they drove on. I said to Gail, "Suppose they had stopped and come after me about this?" She said, "I would have taken care of everything." I said then, this is the woman I need to marry.

The fact was, this little girl used to drive a truck—a huge, working truck—in her youth, her teen years. I thought, Well, good gosh, if she could go out and flip these fellas around, then I've got a bodyguard.

[A few more people told about themselves and then it was Helen's turn.]

Helen: Well, I'm not married—and it's a good thing, because I couldn't do the jobs that I do now. And I'm like John, I wouldn't trade it for anything else there is to do. ECK doesn't let you rest when It takes you on. You know, I wake up at three o'clock in the morning making notes on some of the things that I have to do. I don't get the floor swept, I don't get the laundry done, and I'm lucky if I have time to fix some food to eat. But, I guess I thrive on this kind of thing because I seem to go strong, and it doesn't seem to make any difference.

I was an artist. I was making good money, read *In My Soul I am Free*, and I said, "That's it! That's where I'm going!" That's where I've been ever since. [Author's note: As of this writing, that's where she still is, on the job for ECK.]

Of course, it took a while before they let me work for them, but that was wise too, because it took me that long to really get to a point where I could take the things that happen to you after you start working this close to the Master.

Paulji: I suppose that Helen got probably the roughest treatment of anybody that's been in this work. I would let her have something, and I would withdraw it, and I'd push it forward again, and I'd withdraw it. I'd call her up sometimes at one o'clock in the morning, and I'd say, "Helen, this is what I want done," and bing, bing, bing, bing, bing. She'd say, "Yessir," and I'd always get it done. And then I might call her the next night and say, "No, I don't want that, I've changed my mind." She was confused and frustrated.

But the point is: She stayed in there, and she didn't let this sort of thing bother her. This is important to everybody that's in ECK. Sometimes I'll say I want some things done, and sometimes I'll say it indirectly, and sometimes I'll be very blunt and very forceful about it. But I don't think it's the sort of attitude that should bother anybody. It never bothered her. She went right on and did the job. Maybe she'd do the hard work of a job, and I'd say, "I don't want it."

Now, this isn't all the time, because I'm getting more consistent in my thinking in ECK, where I'm going and our goals. But don't let this sort of thing bother you. Don't be thrown by what I say, because a lot of times I'll throw out things to find out where people are, to see if people are going to be with us, if they're going to stay. Because, if they don't go through these sorts of things and they're not going to stay, they might as well know it now. If this is the end of the road, they might as well make their decision that they aren't going any further. Okay, all right, Patti, you're next.

Patti: Well, I'm very married. I have four kids and I think I spent about the first thirty years of my life bored to death.

When I got into ECK, I was a skeptic. I guess a good word is a doubter. It was interesting enough that I'd sign up and go along with this guy Paulji to see what he had to say, but that's all—just go along with it. And I think I went along like that for a good solid year before it hit me that I was *in* It. It just snuck up on me, really, that's all I can tell you.

But now what's happened is that little by little, piece by piece by piece, It has slowly worked Its way through my life until I don't think that there are five minutes of any day that I'm not either working for or thinking about ECK.

In fact, my husband is not in ECK. One time he was giving me some static, and I said, "Well, would you like me to quit?" And he said, "There wouldn't be anything left of you if you did." And that's pretty much how it is.

I remarked to somebody in my class the other day about how, in my early studies, I used to work so hard on all these principles. For instance, balance. Emotionally, I swung this way [I made a huge pendulum motion with my hand], and I really enjoyed it. I liked those highs. Balance sounded very dull and boring. Then I came to the place where anything but balance is just not acceptable. Balance isn't work anymore. I guess that's what I try to do with all the students I work with: get them to that point where it isn't work anymore. I consider it work if you have anything else going on besides what you're supposed to be doing. Paulji has been giving a lot of his work to me to do lately, which makes life even more interesting and happy for me.

Paulji: Well, Patti's taking over the publications, the two magazines that we're running: the monthly and the quarterly. She's working very closely with me on these. And Patti went through the same thing Helen went through. I almost drove her up the wall. And yet, you know, Patti stayed in there. This is the one thing which everybody has to have, this stamina. If you don't have stamina, you can't take the spiritual life.

You study the lives of all the saints, you look at their lives, and think, Oh, these fellows lived in heaven all the time. They didn't live in heaven all the time. They usually had bigger problems than everybody else — because either the authorities were after them, or they were doing jobs like St. Jerome. They appointed him to do the job of translating the Bible into Latin, the Vulgate. The man spent all these years — I don't know — maybe fifteen years doing this.

Think of poring over all this stuff by candlelight for fifteen years! Think of all the problems the man had — the physical problems. He had to work despite arthritis because the Pope told him to do it.

I want to say one more thing, and I'm going to close here; we're half an hour over. You'd be amazed at the love that exists in ECK between the chelas. I like that because it's not all poured upon me, but it's poured upon one another — and this is good. I have never seen, at any time, anywhere in my life, this sort of spirit existing between one another. This is the balance that I've always preached. When you hold this balance, things aren't going to upset you. Okay, that's all for now.

After we returned to California, I was still holding the love Paulji spoke of, but I wasn't sure about the promise that things weren't going to upset me. I was feeling tired and a bit burned out. When I got home, I felt the need for a rest. Paulji had us planning a meeting for the West Coast youth for early August, and I had my publication deadlines. Suddenly it seemed to me that I really didn't want to do any more than that.

It was about this time that I experienced the feeling I described earlier of having an ocean above me, pouring itself on me, and I had merely a small bucket to catch it all. For whatever reason, I decided to put down my small bucket and rest awhile.

This was not easy: My phone rang every day, and every day my mailbox was full of large brown manila envelopes and blue letter-sized ones addressed in black felt-tip pen. Every call, every letter brought a new task. One day a letter from Paulji arrived in which he outlined my responsi-

272

bilities in ECKANKAR. He had sent a copy of this to the office manager in Las Vegas for his information. This letter was typed, single spaced, and took up *two full pages*. Just reading it made me tired. I think it's important to say here that at no time had I taken a dime in compensation from ECKANKAR. Everything I was doing was strictly as a volunteer. I even paid for all the envelopes, stamps, and stationery, and I wrote literally thousands of letters for Paulji during that time. It was my choice. I liked it that way. I felt that what I was learning and gaining far outweighed the sacrifice of time and money I was investing. And it gave me a certain measure of freedom, because if I didn't feel like working, I had the choice to stop whenever I wanted to, as long as I met my deadlines.

Now I felt like stopping. I did what I have always referred to as "my running away time." This mainly involved getting away from the telephone. As soon as the family got off in the morning, I dressed and raced out to my car. I went to the beach. I went to museums and shopping malls, and I visited with friends. I sat in libraries in cities all over southern California. Each day there was a new thing I would plan, and I would escape the house before the phone could ring. I didn't come home until the deadline, after which Paulji wouldn't call. The letters still came every day. Several times one or another of the kids would tell me he had called but left no message.

I was having a wonderful time. I seemed to be

so free, so light, and so just ME. I knew he was trying to reach me. I knew I was going to have to come back pretty soon, but I was not ready, and when I was, it would all be okay.

My husband, Pete, sensed that I needed rest and recreation. So he planned a trip, one of our favorite things — a few days in San Francisco. I packed with excitement. Now I would really be away from the phone, the mailbox, the kids, everything. I could completely relax and enjoy myself.

We had a flight out of Los Angeles airport, an hour's drive from our home. The baby-sitter was in place, and we set off for our adventure. We were passing the Orange County airport and driving in the fast lane when we began to pass a very large truck which was stopped in the right lane beside us. Suddenly, as our vehicle reached the intersection beside the truck, a car darted out from a side street, which was hidden by the huge truck. By the time we saw it, it was broadside to us; and although there was a horrendous screeching of brakes, we smashed into the car, hitting the door on the driver's side. For us, it was head on.

For those who have never been in an automobile accident and seen it coming, I'd like to say that in the fraction of a second between the time you know you're going to hit and the actual impact, you seem to be able to accommodate a large body of realizations. I don't know of any other endeavor in which we are able to think about so much so fast. In the space of that minute fraction of time, I thought three things:

1. There goes our trip to San Francisco.
2. There goes my neck again.
3. Ohhhhhhh, noooooooo!
   KERBLAMMM

Actually, the last word I thought may have been more colorful than no.

When it was all sorted out, the truck driver had actually been the culprit. He had stopped in such a way at the intersection that he caused a blind spot for the driver of the other car, a young woman. She couldn't see around his truck. She said he had signaled to her that it was clear for her to enter the intersection. Of course, it was all clear except for us, driving happily along. And, *of course,* the truck driver didn't see us because, no doubt, Patti needed to have an automobile accident that day. As in most collisions of this sort, the truck driver was well down the road before the last piece of broken glass landed in the street.

There was no blood anywhere. Miraculously, the lady who took our broadside wasn't hurt, nor was my husband. Only me. I sat there shaking with despair and holding my newly whiplashed neck.

In order for the reader to understand the depths of my despair, I should give a brief history of this injury. Whiplash is one of those injuries that seems to stay with you for years. One may have no symptoms, then when one is under stress, or is fatigued, or has even been sleeping in the wrong position, the whole thing can come back with its original intensity. Since I had already had two whiplash injuries, I was in a more or less constant battle with the symptoms.

Before this most recent accident, the doctors had already tried just about everything on me: neck collars, hot fomentations, traction, muscle relaxants, etc. I would get better for a while, but anything could trigger a new disability, even gardening. Through my association with ECKANKAR, I had then met a doctor who used a combination of chiropractic and acupressure. It brought the most relief I had ever had. I had had very few episodes of whiplash symptoms after he began to work on the problem, and I was beginning to entertain the hope that I might even achieve a permanent cure.

The day after the accident, my husband began a series of trips, driving me to the doctor's house. I was going to need intensive treatment, Doc said, and if I got it now, the usual whiplash residue could probably be avoided. Now I had a legitimate excuse not to be home to answer the phone, and I was well into my third week of not being at home whenever Paulji called.

Doc wanted to do a series of treatments, I believe it was three in twenty-four hours. In order to avoid all the driving, the doctor and his wife arranged for me to spend the night at their house. Since they were also going to have their Satsang Class that evening, they said I was more than welcome to join them. Doc gave me one treatment when I arrived. I was to have another after the

Satsang Class, and a third the following morning.

That evening the members of the class arrived and I joined them. A short time after the discussion began, the phone rang and Doc excused himself to answer it. I knew. I *knew* who it was. Who else always called in the middle of a Satsang Class? After a while Doc came back in the room and interrupted the discussion. "Uh, Patti, you're wanted on the phone."

I sighed in resignation, went into the other room, and picked up the phone. "Hi Paulji." He said that Doc had told him about my accident. He was very nice, telling me to take it easy, etc. He then talked about some of my projects. Before long, he was onto the American Civil War and the War of 1812, which wasn't really in 1812, he said. I smiled as I listened to all this, but I was weary and in pain — and greatly relieved when he finally hung up. I made it back to the Satsang Class in time to bid them all good-bye. It was not a new experience.

I held out against Paulji about one more week. And in this period of time I really needed the break, since I was really too sick to do much else. Sitting at the typewriter was agony, and I kept it to the minimum. Mostly, I got in my car and kept running from Paulji.

Then one day I found a blue envelope in the mailbox with a very terse note. It was written on half a piece of letter-sized stationery, which had a torn, ragged edge on the right. On one side it said, "Patti: Get another printer. This *Monthly Letter* should have never gone out. Errors and pixs are too bad. You must have done this after your accident — PT." On the back of this was a post-script: "P.S. I never seem to get you by telephone anymore. Won't call again since it's only costing calls — If you want me, please call — PT."

I read this postscript several times, and a grin spread over my face. I don't know what it was all about. I didn't really know why I had run away, nor why it was suddenly all over now. Holding back outright laughter, I broke my silent rule: I dialed up Paulji's number. When he answered, I said, "Hi! I'm back!" We had a fine conversation, full of the old banter, and whatever it was all about was completely over, finished. Neither of us ever spoke of it again.

As for the whiplash, I continued to suffer sporadic episodes of the symptoms until around 1974, about the time I received my Eighth Initiation. At that time, I met Wai Wan, a marvelous Chinese doctor from Shanghai. Wai Wan gave me eight acupuncture treatments in three weeks. I have not suffered whiplash pain for ten years — not until I began to approach this part of my story. Now that my pen and my body have remembered it all for this document, perhaps I will once again be "cured."

Twenty

In the middle of July 1971, Paulji and
Gail went to Seattle, Washington, for a
family visit. At this point in our association,
Paulji and I had achieved a high degree of mutual
trust and were as relaxed with each other as we
would ever be. Whatever had caused my "running
away time," it precipitated another change in our
relationship. Now, for the first time, I felt that
Paulji considered me not only his chela, assistant,
and biographer, but also his friend. This was the
newest and last honor he was to bestow on me. It
was a rare occurrence for Paulji to bestow such a
personal honor upon anyone.

While he and Gail were gone, several packages
had arrived in the mail. They were tape cassettes
that he had recorded for the biography while in
Seattle. Since some of the most important events
in his mission had taken place in Seattle, I know
that he welcomed the trip as an opportunity to jolt

many of the facts out of his memory. The tapes are a wonderful rendering of his zanier, eccentric, and carefree days as a newspaper reporter on the *Post-Intelligencer,* and of the terrible struggle he underwent to achieve the state of spiritual mastership. Written on the cassette was the brief title: "For Patti — Struggle for the Mastership."

Listening to these tapes was a moving experience. Paulji had already mentioned his many illnesses and near-death experiences as a child. He had been very prone to pneumonia and had been critically ill with it at least once. These grave times had left him with a speech impediment, which left him shy and a loner. Could the Masters of the Vairagi possibly have picked a candidate whose temperment was more ill-suited to be the new Mahanta? Certainly they couldn't have found one more reluctant. But the task was his to do. The speech impediment had to be overcome. The aversion to crowds and the desire to be alone had to be overcome. The years of research and study of the spiritual dynamics had to be organized and systematized. Somehow he did it.

Now, when we worked, he was completely relaxed with the tape recorder running. He realized that he never knew what he was going to say, or when he would suddenly lapse into this greater consciousness and put into motion or record something that was a direct manifestation of the Mahanta Consciousness in operation. He once said, "It will help us to see how this thing works."

Often during these days, I found Paulji doing

something that fascinated me. Letters would come in from all over telling him about things he had done in his inner light form, and of the miraculous changes brought about in others' lives. He did not, as one might imagine, shrug it off as a thing he already knew. He himself seemed to be studying it, learning its dynamics and how it worked, with every bit as much fascination as I. People often wrote or told me of their experiences with this inner form: healings, miraculous escapes from certain death, resolutions of family problems, the taking across of some loved one at the moment of physical death. They saw and experienced these things. Paulji would listen intently and smile when I related the stories to him. Sometimes he would explain some factor in the story with a statement like, "Well, the way this thing works . . ." Except in his writings and lectures, in which he used the proper terminology, he referred to the Mahanta Consciousness as "this thing," and he referred to his function as the Living ECK Master as either "this job" or "this work."

I came across a tape which illustrates one such incident. I had just told Paulji the story, which I told in detail in *Hello Friend*, about the woman whose divorced husband had a visit from Paulji in Arizona (he had had no idea who Paulji was). This visitor in blue told him to seek out his ex-wife and try the marriage again, as they had unfinished karma between them.

The man came to California to find her and pursue a reconciliation. When he found her, he saw her wallet open on the table. In it was a picture of Paulji; the very man who had visited him. The man demanded to know his name, and she reluctantly told him it was Paul Twitchell, her spiritual guide. As was often the case with these experiences, Paulji was physically in San Diego at the time the man saw and talked with him in Arizona. Recently remarried, the couple had come to my home and told me this story; and I had written a letter to Paulji about it, which he refers to in the following edited conversation.

Paulji: You know, that was a very interesting letter you sent me the other day about this fellow going to marry this woman. I was out in Arizona—went to Arizona.

Patti: Isn't that something? That woman has faith, let me tell you. She said, "Patti, you have no idea what it took for me to stand up in front of that preacher, knowing that I do not love this man, but it's something that I have to do." And she married him. Did you see that letter, Gail?

[She nods.]

Paulji to Gail: You stick around friend and you'll find out who I am.

Patti: . . . and what's going on.

Gail: . . . and where you've been.

[There is laughter.]

Paulji: What do you call those things: the Wampus Birds? They fly backwards because they don't care where they're going, they just want to

282

see where they've been. Did you ever hear that one?

Patti: So, you wait for the mail to find out where you've been.

Paulji: Always catching up.

Patti: Well, this sort of thing goes on all the time. I feel that this has to be kept track of and put together in a book. We've got to do something with it.

Paulji: Well, people don't pay enough attention to the inner things that are happening to them. They always have to be thinking about the outer things.

I had come to the point where I didn't even notice the paranormal happenings. Had I gotten myself caught up in them, it would have taken too much of my time and attention. I began to simply take a lot of it for granted, so that today, when I hear these "miracle" stories, they often seem no more miraculous to me than any other story.

A few months prior to this writing I was doing a workshop with some ECK students and one of the people asked me about this. The question went something like, "When one reaches the Eighth Circle of Initiation, doesn't one live more or less in the *Nirvikalpa,* or a continual state of bliss?" Although my reply may have been a little disappointing to him, I told him that a continual state of bliss is really not a terribly high state of consciousness, and that whatever state of consciousness I have achieved, I don't seem to be going high and low: but everything *is,* here and now. And it seems to me that the experiences that once caught my breath as miraculous and phenomenal are now merely part of an expanded awareness of all of the possibile realities. At first they are remarkable, I suppose, as a jet plane is remarkable to a native in a remote rain forest, but once the native moves into the consciousness of the era of jet planes, they are not even noticed anymore.

I had an appointment to go to Paulji's house on August 3, which was my birthday. It was going to be a short session with lunch because there was a dinner celebration planned at home. However, I didn't tell Paulji any of this, only that I had another appointment later.

We had our regular business meeting and then he took Gail and me out to the usual restaurant in La Jolla for lunch. Then we returned to the house and chatted for a short while. Paulji and I had a discussion about the value of the tapes we were doing, and how the office manager was having a difficult time about our doing this. I had written a report to him about the taping and that Paulji was to be taped by someone else if I wasn't there. I didn't think he understood what I was talking about. Paulji laughed. [Here is our edited conversation.]

Paulji: He taped some when he was down here, and I said, "Well, the problem with all of this is we're getting the consciousness of heading for

284

the deceased state! Everybody's grabbing on the last words I'm saying.

Gail: Taking down your last words.

Paulji: I'll probably be like the fellow I knew who was in his last, dying state. He opened his mouth to say something and everybody gathered in real close, y'know, to find out what he was going to say. And he says, "Turn off all those lights—it's costing too much money!"

Patti: Well, I'll say one thing—I've got a lot of tapes. I've got this drawer, and it's about half-full. I had to explain to the office manager how I've seen things evolve through these tapes. I wouldn't have even gotten the insights on some of these things but for ideas that developed from a first little conversation here. The ideas grow and grow until eventually they will even come out as a message.

Paulji: Right.

Patti: And which are documented by tapes.

Paulji: Do you know, you are talking about a very interesting thing. I go around here a lot of times and I'm thinking so loud—now, I'm not talking, but thinking very loud. One time I was standing in there looking out the window, and I was thinking about saying something in one of these seminars about having a dog and a wife and two teddy bears—and you people think you've got troubles. And I was just thinking this, kind of going over it, and Gail comes in and she says, "What about a dog and two teddy bears?"

See, now, often she'll do that and I haven't opened my mouth. And it's real peculiar because it starts developing something, see? She'll say, "Oh, what do you want to talk about that for?" Then I'll say, "Well, I don't know." And it's just going like it was a regular conversation, as if I'd sat down and talked to her about it — it just develops into a regular conversation.

And I have told her so much, I doubt if she'll ever remember it — about childhood and everything. For instance, the other day I was telling a real interesting story pertaining to our family. My stepbrother was really an efficient fellow in business. He was a hard worker. He went to school; they sent him off to seminary school, a Baptist institute. He stayed there a year and then he went to a military college, a prep school, in Virginia. He bounced all around those places. He went to the university and stayed two years.

He was in love with a girl and said he was going to come back and marry her. She said if he didn't finish school, she wasn't going to have anything to do with him. A very funny thing about this girl — her name was Sexton, and they all — everybody — called her Sexy. [Laughs] She really was a marvelous girl. I liked her; she was a tremendous girl.

But, my stepbrother came on back anyway. He went down to the riverdocks, where he had been working during the summer, and went in as a welder. My dad was the superintendent of the place.

Now, mind you, in those days he could make fifty dollars a week as a welder, if he'd work hard and overtime. They were changing over from the wooden hulls to the steel-hulled boats, and that was his job, welding.

The yard foreman, who handled the whole works, was very fond of my stepbrother. He took him under his wing and taught him how to do blueprints and draw up plans for building boats, and everything else. My stepbrother took one of those international correspondence courses in engineering and blueprinting, and he got very good at that. And when the yard foreman died, my stepbrother was put up for his job.

But first, before that, I forgot that they had a big flood — a huge flood that washed out everything. The Chicago office of the company, which was an international company, sent a CPA to become office manager. He took one look at that place after the flood and quit. Said he didn't want it and went back to his original job. So my stepbrother was put into the job and he had to become a bookkeeper. At that time he went out in the yard and helped with the planning of the building and everything. The company had given my stepbrother six months — told him if he made it in six months, he could have the job.

Well, he made it. World War II came along and the company sent him to Washington D. C. to make government bids. Whoever got the lowest bid got to repair and do the building for the government with the Coast Guard of all the government river equipment that hauled oil and everything up and down the river.

So, he went up there and what did he do? He made the *highest* bid; he wouldn't make the lowest bid. He naturally lost the bid with the government, and his company called him to Pittsburgh and said, "Well, look, what's wrong with you? Are you crazy?" He said, "No, I'm not crazy. There are four yards, four big shipyards, up and down the Ohio and the Mississippi that have the government stuff. The contract reads that they could only do government work. Who's going to repair the rest of the equipment on the river? I'll bet you from the time we start tomorrow that we will be loaded down with independent repair."

And they were. They made a fortune out of it— an absolute fortune. That made him a big man in the company, and the company sold out all the big river equipment.

And that is exactly why we kept the tape recorder going. Something would start out as a rather innocuous conversation, and bingo, more biographical data would come streaming forth.

After this exchange, Paulji got up and left the room. Gail and I continued our conversation. All of a sudden, behind me, I heard a little, squeaky, high-pitched voice singing. I looked around, and walking toward me, singing "Happy Birthday to Patti" in this soft little voice, was Paulji. He was in his stocking feet, holding a lovely ceramic planter filled with houseplants. I was completely taken by surprise. I don't have any idea how they found out it was my birthday, and they had both kept this secret all through the day. Before he had finished his song, the tape recorder ran out of tape. I was so touched, so wondrously moved, that I was near tears. To cover my emotions, I joked: "Gee, that's got to be a historic moment. How about singing it again after I turn over the tape?" He said that his singing voice was not particularly a thing he would be remembered for. However, that does not hold true for at least one person. I will treasure that moment forever.

The plants grew and grew and grew. I had to take them out of the tiny planter and repot them. Over the years, one by one, they have disappeared, all except for a little palm tree, which was about two-and-a-half inches tall when he gave it to me. Today, it sits in a pot in my entry hall and is about a foot tall.

When I moved to my present home, I thought the little palm would love the out-of-doors. I planted it in a garden right next to the window, so that every time I passed, I would see it. However, I discovered that it was getting scrawnier and scrawnier and was down to only two fronds. As I began this book, I went to look at it, to meditate upon those times and use it as a catalyst for my thoughts. It looked so ill and forlorn that I immediately went down to the store and bought a nice pot. I dug it out of the garden, repotted it, and now it sits on the *inside* of that same window. I was very worried about its survival and fed it some Bach

Flower Rescue Remedy and vitamins, and sent it good thoughts. In some ways, that is a reflection of what has been going on in these pages. I am very happy to report that in the past few weeks, the little palm has begun growing a new frond. No doubt, about the time this is published, it will be fully open. Life works that way.

When I left San Diego on my birthday in 1971, I was filled with gentle happiness. It was truly a wondrous thing that I was doing such interesting, exciting work, and had two such friends as Paulji and Gail. The only tiny speck to mar the perfection of the day was a slight uneasiness: Paulji seemed to be making more and more references to his death these days.

Twenty-One

A week after my surprise birthday party, the Inner Circle gathered again — this time at the Edgewater Hotel in Long Beach, California — for another Youth Workshop. This was the third such meeting in four months. This particular gathering was primarily composed of young people from the west coasts of the United States and Canada.

Paulji refused to be scheduled for this group and elected to drop in whenever he felt like it. This was a real challenge, keeping all of us on our toes, because we never knew when he would suddenly pop in the door. He was very relaxed and usually showed up wearing pale blue cotton slacks, a blue cotton work shirt and, to everyone's delight, pale blue tennis shoes.

His opening talk was a typically relaxed affair. It almost seemed to be an unfocused stream of consiousness, until one looked more closely. He was putting into perspective what was happening in the ECKANKAR movement. The following transcript is edited to make reading easier.

"I hate to start early because just about the time I get started, in comes a group of people.

"Well, all right, if you can't hear me in the back would you please raise your hand? All right, I'll lift up my voice a little.

"We called the West Coast group together because we're now moving into new areas and new directions. I feel that there are a lot of new ideas springing up in the world which have to do with the human element, as well as the spiritual element.

"We are now beginning to appeal to a new type of audience. I'm finding that all over the country more people in the younger age bracket are beginning to find ECK, and it sets up new directions and new forces and new ideas. I think that these should be incorporated into ECK. We've got more and more expansion because I would not put it in a strait jacket. Now, for example, I say that the majority of ideas that go on in these fields of religions and philosophy have narrowed themselves down to a very narrow path. I can be a Christian or I can be a Moslem, I can be almost anything, but then I'm put into a strait jacket. Should people ask me what I am and I say, 'Well, I'm Jewish,' immediately the other minds will put me into this slot and I become one of the many that go around the outside circle of which ECK is the hub. All of these religions and philosophies are the spokes which flow out from ECK, and ECK is all-embracing of them.

"So, what we have to begin to think about — and I'm guilty of this point myself — is that we can't really say that ECK is even a path. It embraces so much of life because It is life itself. The only thing we're doing is using certain exercises and certain ideas in order to open ourselves to this flow — or whatever you want to call It, that is coming into us — or we are traveling out to It. So we find that we are embracing the whole of everything and not a small, narrow path. And the minute that we begin to put ourselves into this narrow path, we have failed, because we then put ourselves on another path.

"Ever since we have been in the work, either I or someone else has repeated that our minds should be vastly broadened and deepened so that we know we are not another path. We can't be put into a category. We are It, of Itself. When you are out in the field and are talking to people, someone will say, 'Oh, you are like yoga, or Vedanta, or Christianity,' or any of these things. They try to make a comparison because they've never actually had the whole. We are thinking about the whole, and they are thinking about the parts. You must remember, that when one thinks in the parts, he puts everything in a category. When one thinks in the whole, he thinks of all of it.

"Now, all these individual parts that we are speaking about have saviors, all have founders.

293

We don't deny that. We don't deny the validity of what they did for their particular teaching or the validity of those people who became their disciples. These individual parts became worldwide movements like Hinduism or Buddhism. But then, you begin to wonder when you look at all of these works. For instance, Buddhism was the reform of the Hindu religion. Take Christ, if you want to put him in the same light, he was a reformer of the Jewish religion.

"Have you ever stopped to think about the restrictions that those people had at one time? The Hindu had the same. I think on Sabbath the Jewish person could only walk fifty feet from where he had stopped on Friday night. He could only eat certain things that day, and he could not do any daily chores. Everything was restricted right down into a very small unit. Out of this grew the reformers, who said, 'Why put all these restrictions upon yourselves?' And they began to do the reforming. And what happened? Krishna did it in Hinduism and was killed. Christ was slain. All of these people usually go out because the society doesn't like them. They're up against the establishment, and it gets rid of them one way or another.

"Buddha, I think, had a little easier time of it. He, of course, died of his own volition, because somebody, unknowingly, gave him poisoned rice to eat. He was told by his own disciples, 'You know, the food is tainted.' And he said, 'Yes, I know it is, but this is the only thing that the man has to give me, so how can I refuse it?' And this brought about his death.

"Now, these things are the essence of the works in the part. So, as we are working in the whole, we have to begin to think about ourselves individually, and how we can handle ourselves with the public. More and more people are learning about ECKANKAR, and they're coming to you saying, 'What is it? What does it mean?' And this is why we have been calling in youth groups across the country, because we want you to be able to communicate with such people when they start asking these questions.

"I'm reminded of a friend of ours in ECK. I suppose she's middle-aged, in her mid-fifties, rather. Well, she got quite disturbed one day because our attention had turned to the youth. So she was asked, 'Do you think you're going to live forever?' And that stopped her, see, because we don't. And one day, you'll be in the same position, and you'll be talking to the next generation. If we don't, then we're dead. And we might as well give it up and all go back in our own little corners and study individually.

"Now, there is one point we've got to make, and it is a strange factor. This is the factor of the death wish. I'm giving you a little death psychology here because it may be that you never thought about it before. At your age you're not thinking too much of death, because you're in the exuberance of youth. You're happy. And if you're thinking about death, then there's something wrong. Although when I was your age, I was

295

thinking about it; but I was a little morbid and a little more romantic. I think romance goes with death. [Paulji tells the story of *Wuthering Heights*.]

"The point I'm trying to give you is the whole human race, not the human race alone, but everything that's in the physical flesh today is very conscious of this death wish. It is in us from the time of our birth to the time of death. In some people it's greater and in others it's less. As one grows older, the same thing happens. Occasionally we find an elderly man who's very happy and getting along, and he's not thinking about any of this, but the majority of people are. We have this within us, and this is a big factor in the human race. The ECK, of Itself, is the great factor of survival.

"If you read the newspapers, it's a very interesting thing to see. They are all filled with this negative sort of thing. Children in schools get it in literature. They're told to prepare fast to get to a career because one day you're coming to that point where you have to have a family and then you see them grow up and then you have to die. Those are the facts that are put into us in school. For my part, I don't see why they couldn't have been a little bit more cheerful and a little more happy about the situation. But in ECK we know that we have survival, and this is the wonderful thing about this: we know that when we have to leave this world, then we go into other planes, and we've got the beautiful experience of knowing

296

this. When we think that this is the end of life, then we have missed the whole point of ECK. We don't stop at this life. We go on into eternity as the individual.

"These are some of the things I talk about when I talk to other people who seem to have a degree of reasonableness, when I'm not trying to break through a hard shell. Anybody that came to me and was hard-shelled and wanted arguments, I wouldn't be bothered with him; it's not going to win anything anyway. And believe me, I have this to say, that the row which we have to hoe will not be as easy as we think it will be.

"I had the first six or seven years of it and carried it all on my shoulders. Now we're delegating to people out in the field. If anybody would ask me if I would go through it again, I would say, "Yes, I would go through it, but I would always feel a little dread of what's going to happen." If I had to go out and make it known to the world again, I'd have new ideas, and I'd have new approaches, of course. But I just had to dig the ground as it came. And, believe me, it was good experience. It put me in the position of being able to have the answers."

[Paulji then begins to tell the story of a Ronald Coleman movie in which Coleman played a great vagabond poet of France during the twelfth century.]

"They had him in prison and were going to behead him over something, and here he was, making beautiful poetry, walking around and reciting it. The next day he was going to his grave. Some of the others asked him, 'Well, what gives here? How can you recite and make up beautiful poetry at this moment when you're coming to the end of your life?' He said, 'What greater inspiration is there?' So [Paul laughs], sometimes I feel that way too. I get down here at the end of everything—and nothing more—and I feel like I can get up and recite poetry, because this is the time of inspiration for it."

[Paulji then tells the young people the story of his growing up, how many people he saw die who had no understanding of the survival of Soul, and of his own struggle to find some place for himself in life.]

"And this is why I finally, after all my wandering around, suddenly discovered that there was something moving me all the time, moving me into the position for all of this. All of it was training; I was being trained for something. We should never waste one experience in our life—any experience. Every experience should be a lesson; it should be that which we take and build upon—and know this has a purpose, regardless of what it might be...."

Paulji's lecture went on much longer. He covered a great deal of territory, and at least two more times he got into the subject of death.

In the almost fourteen years since he left this plane, I have not listened to this tape or read the transcript. As I did so now, I was astonished to see that right there, in front of all of us, he was winding it up. I did not see it at the time, nor, do I believe, did anyone else who was there. He so beautifully tied all these thoughts into the survival of Soul, the basic tenet of ECKANKAR, that we all took this to be merely another factor of his teaching.

There were many meetings in his and Gail's rooms. Planning was in full swing for the Fifth World Wide Seminar coming up in Las Vegas in October. We also had our lunches together with the usual stories and laughter. It was a gentle time, a time of sharing and of feeling good about things.

One afternoon I sat in a meeting of the young people as an observer. They were running the meeting and were filled with plans and projects and stories of their lives and how they got here. Suddenly, a great calm came over me, and I seemed to switch into another mode of consciousness. It was a kind of realization. What I could see was a vision far into the future. ECKANKAR was going to make it. It was established on this plane. Nothing would stop it now. It was a Knowing.

Late that afternoon I was in Paulji's room talking with him about the program, and I told him about my experience. He had gone into the bedroom to get his shoes, preparatory to our going out to dinner. He stood there in the doorway, his shoes in his hands, and said to me very quietly: "You will never know — no one will ever know — what a struggle it's been."

He said this wearily and, as I looked at his face,

I saw that incredible weariness etched in deep lines. He was tired, through and through.

Several weeks later, I got a blue envelope in the mail. Inside was a handwritten letter and another envelope.

Sept 10/'71

Dear Patti:

For the sake of posterity here's a PT relic — with all the magical properties which go with it —

When you build your altar, you can put a lock of this hair in it — for the sake of making it personal and close to me and for expected miracles!

It's a good thing I don't have blue hair or I might be bald from giving away hair — or I could dye it, should this mean anything —

PT

P.S. I hope no chelas will start demanding any bones as souvenirs while I'm still among the living — I'd dislike missing a finger or toe just because somebody desire[d] either —

In the second envelope, sure enough, was a lock of his hair. I did not know what to make of it. He was, I thought, probably kidding around. Maybe he'd been reading a book about some of these artifacts from the old times or something. I put it away and didn't want to think about it.

On the fourteenth of September, I was once again at his house. We had a regular work session prior to his trip to Cincinnati, which was coming up in two days. There was really nothing out of the ordinary about it, except that when I arrived there was a note from Gail on the front door. It said:

> Patti —
> Come in —
> Wake Paul,
> if necessary —
> Have a good
> day!
> G.

I was standing there on the front porch trying to figure out what in the world to do. If Paulji was still asleep, I didn't want to ring the bell and disturb him. There was no way I was going to walk in, find his bedroom, and wake him up. It was out of the question. Thoughts of the gardener running his power mower remained firmly embedded in my mind, so I didn't do anything. I simply stood there wondering what to do. All of a sudden the door opened and there stood Paulji, wide awake and fully dressed. He invited me in and I showed him Gail's note. He exploded into laughter. "Well, that's Gail for you," he said. Apparently, it hadn't occurred to Gail that, friend or not, asking a chela to go into the Master's bedroom and wake him up was really an awkward situation. Paulji loved it!

We went ahead with our regular work session. Then we went out to eat and shortly after, I left. During the whole time we were together, I never mentioned the letter with the hair in it. I simply couldn't bring myself to talk about it. It seemed there was a whole subject lingering beneath the surface that we couldn't talk about. It was an unspoken contract; it was untouchable.

He was breaking with pattern on this trip. On his seminar trips he always took either Helen, me, or Gail, or any combination of the three. This time he was going without any of us and taking another ECKist instead. It was strange, indeed.

The night before he was due to leave, the fifteenth, the phone rang at about eight o'clock. It was Paulji. He said he'd just called up to say goodbye; he was leaving in the morning. This struck me as terribly odd. He had never, never, in all the time I'd known him, called my house at night. He sounded tired and was grumbling that he didn't really want to go. I said, "Paulji," and then whatever it was that I was going to say was wiped so totally from my mind that I was completely blank.

"Yes, Patti?" he prompted. I started laughing.

"You know, Paulji, it's the weirdest thing. I was going to say something to you, but it was suddenly erased from my mind. I am a complete blank."

He laughed. And I laughed. But I was frowning and wondering what had happened. Paulji mentioned feeling very tired, so I kidded him a little.

"Why don't you just put on your pajamas? Don't forget to safety pin the shirt, pull up a blanket, and tell the stewardess not to bother you until you're in Cincinnati."

He chuckled, saying that was not a bad idea.
Then we said good-bye.

The next night, at one-thirty a.m., California
time, I got the call that said Paulji had translated in
Cincinnati. The people could not get Gail on the
phone and asked me to keep trying to reach her to
let her know. I stayed up the rest of the night trying
to contact her, not knowing that she was out of
town. At four-thirty in the morning, I scribbled a
letter to myself and to all the powers that be.

Sept. 17, 1971
4:30 a.m.

He's gone — Master — Mahanta —
beloved friend — Left the scarred
battered vehicle — left us — all
on this plane. Tears sting and
spill out unashamedly — not
because he is gone — he isn't really, but
maybe because the phone won't
ever ring again when I'll hear
that voice say "Well, Miss Patti —
What's new?"

I miss you —
my friend — and through
my human tears — you've
earned them — I have
the inner knowing you're
here — and always will be —
It's that silent phone for
which I weep —

303

> Oh, how will I tell
> Gail? I ask Mahanta please
> give me what it takes to
> help her through — and me
> through — and all my spiritual
> brothers and sisters through —

By early morning, I was exhausted from my efforts to call Gail. Finally I telephoned the local police department in Del Mar and explained the problem. I asked them to put a note on her front door which merely requested her to call me when she got home.

Gail did call and before I even had a chance to say anything she said, "It's Paul, isn't it? He's gone." I said, "Yes." Gail told me that she had known it was going to happen. She'd been camping in the mountains with friends. In the night, lying there in her sleeping bag under the stars, she had known.

Gail did a magnificent job of accepting what had to be. She had never really been on her own since college, and now she put all Paulji had taught her into action. She dealt with life as if it were not the least bit frightening, but a challenge and a chance for her to try her wings. If she were not *really* Mighty Mouse before, she certainly was then.

In the fourteen years since his translation, Paulji has come around now and then — not often, but always when I really needed his counsel. But in the early days, right after he left, he was around frequently. Gail and I had many experiences with him and many messages. One of the neatest ones involved his safety pin.

Ever since he was a child with so many problems with chest congestion, he'd had to have his pajama tops closed up to his throat. To his annoyance, none of them would button high enough for him, so he always safety-pinned them at the neck. He once told me that his stepmother had lost his safety pin, and he had been unable to sleep the entire night. As a gift, Gail had once bought him a solid gold safety pin. He never left on a trip without it. Yet, when his personal effects were sent back from Cincinnati, the gold pin was not among them. Gail was mightily upset about this and wondered if someone, not realizing its importance, and that it was real gold, had thrown it out. Then one day, weeks later, she opened a drawer in the office, and there was Paulji's gold safety pin. She had opened that drawer many times since his translation; the safety pin had not been there.

Around the same time, I lost my car keys at a chela potluck dinner. We looked everywhere for them and didn't find them. I had to use a spare key to get home. Sometime later, I found them under the front seat of my car. But something new had been added. Attached to the key chain was a silver-colored metal thunderbird, the Indian symbol that Paulji was so fond of.

For many years I pondered his strange message that had accompanied the lock of hair: "When you build your altar." They were words that made no sense whatsoever, as we have no such things as altars in ECKANKAR. The part about keeping the lock of hair in my personal altar for expected miracles was easier. I went out and bought a little gold locket and put a few strands of the hair in it, and wore it for a long time; but the chains kept breaking, and it seemed there must be a better way.

I solved it a few years ago when David and I were about to be married. David is also a High Initiate, and we share the same love and dedication to the ECK. Before we were married, we designed our wedding rings: two gold bands with leaf patterns on them, a symbol of our spiritual brotherhood. The rings were to be made in the lost-wax casting process, and the jeweler, a wonderful lady who wasn't the least bit flustered about our unusual request, made arrangements for us to be there when the casting was done. As we stood there watching, the gold became molten; and just before they "threw" it into the cast, we put several strands of Paulji's hair into it. It was a very magic moment and everyone in the workroom felt it, although they had no idea of what had taken place.

And so it is that I keep the lock of hair close to me. The first miracle occurred, I think, when this beautiful Soul and I joined forces in a marriage that has nurtured and supported each of us in everything Soul leads us to explore.

The hour grows late. The story has been told and . . . well, Paulji, I think we ought to take off . . .

The End

ECKANKAR Presents a Spiritual Study Course: *Soul Travel—The Illuminated Way*

People want to know the secrets of life and death. In response to this need Paul Twitchell, the modern-day founder of ECKANKAR, brought to light the Spiritual Exercises of ECK—which offer a direct way to God.

Those who are ready to begin a study of ECKANKAR can receive special monthly discourses which give clear, simple instructions for these exercises. The first twelve-month series is called *Soul Travel—The Illuminated Way*. Mailed each month, the discourses are designed to lead the individual to the Light and Sound of God.

The techniques in these discourses, when practiced twenty minutes a day, are likely to prove survival beyond death. Many have used them as a direct route to Self-Realization, where one learns his mission in life. The next stage, God Consciousness, is the joyful state wherein Soul becomes the spiritual traveler, an agent for God. The underlying principle one learns then is this: "Soul exists because God loves It."

Discourses include these titles, among others: "The Universality of Soul Travel," "The Illuminated Way by Direct Projection," and "The Spiritual Cities of This World." These can be studied at home or with fellow students in a local ECKANKAR class—look in the phone book under ECKANKAR, or write us for classes in your area.

For more information on how to receive *Soul Travel—The Illuminated Way* and ECKANKAR classes in your area, use the coupon at the back of this book, or write:

ECKANKAR, P.O. Box 3100, Menlo Park, CA 94026 U.S.A.

Introductory Books on ECKANKAR

The Wind of Change, Sri Harold Klemp

What are the hidden spiritual reasons behind every event in your life? With stories drawn from his own life-long training, ECKANKAR's spiritual leader shows you how to use the power of Spirit to discover those reasons. Follow him from the Wisconsin farm of his youth, to a military base in Japan; from a job in Texas, into the realms beyond, as he shares the secrets of ECKANKAR.

ECKANKAR—The Key to Secret Worlds, Paul Twitchell

Paul Twitchell, modern-day founder of ECKANKAR, gives you the basics of this ancient teaching. Includes six specific Soul Travel exercises to see the Light and hear the Sound of God, plus case histories of Soul Travel. Learn to recognize yourself as Soul—and journey into the heavens of the Far Country.

The Tiger's Fang, Paul Twitchell

Paul Twitchell's teacher, Rebazar Tarzs, takes him on a journey through vast worlds of Light and Sound, to sit at the feet of the spiritual Masters. Their conversations bring out the secret of how to draw closer to God—and awaken Soul to Its spiritual destiny. Many have used this book, with its vivid descriptions of heavenly worlds and citizens, to begin their own spiritual adventures.

Hello Friend, Patti Simpson

Patti Simpson, long-time student of ECKANKAR, explores this ancient path from the perspective of the spiritual student, covering such questions as: "Do I need a spiritual guide? How can I make the Spiritual Exercises of ECK work for me? What's Soul Travel like?" Patti answers with warmth and humor, drawing stories and examples from rich spiritual experiences.

For more free information about the books and teachings of ECKANKAR, please write: **ECKANKAR, P.O. Box 3100, Menlo Park, CA 94026 U.S.A.**

Or look under ECKANKAR in your local phone book for an ECKANKAR Center near you.

For Free Information on ECKANKAR...

☐ Yes, I want free information on ECKANKAR. Please send me brochures on the ECKANKAR books and on the twelve-month study series, *Soul Travel—The Illuminated Way.*

☐ I would like information on the nearest ECKANKAR discussion or study group in my area.

Please type or print clearly   941

Name_____

Street_____

City_____State/Prov. _____

Zip/Postal Code_____Country_____

(Our policy: Your name and address are held in strict confidence—we do not rent or sell our mailing lists. Nor will we send anyone to call on you.)

ECKANKAR
P.O. Box 3100
Menlo Park, CA 94026
U.S.A.